CW00553990

SPIRITUAL DOWSING

Sig Lonegren

GOTHIC IMAGE
PUBLICATIONS

Lonegren, Sig
SPIRITUAL DOWSING
I.   DOWSING ROD
1.   TITLE
1323.3.'23   BF 1628

ISBN 0-906362-06-7

Typeset by Wordsmiths,
          19, West End,
          Street, Somerset

Printed by Sydney Lee (Exeter) Ltd.,
          Water Lane,
          Exeter, Devon EX2 8DC

Published by Gothic Image Publications,
          7, High Street,
          Glastonbury,
          Somerset BA6 9DP

Cover illustration by Ginnie Graham 1986
Cover design by Jem Jarman 1986

To

Terry Ross

Acknowledgements

As a dyslexic, I have really had to rely on the help of others to spot simple misteaks. I am grateful for the time and energy Dave Travers, Lee Dabney, Virginia and Sally Lonegren, John Miles Evans, and Tom Graves put into reading the manuscript and giving me their thoughts and corrections. I appreciate the work done by Ginnie Graham, Jan Graves, Cath Milne, Chesca Potter, Diana Griffiths, Martin Brennan, and Ian Thompson. Their illustrations illuminate the book in ways that words can not express. Also thanks to Jennifer Cobb for proof-reading the final text. Paul Devereux introduced me to the Earth Mysteries in Britain, and I appreciate his taking me to sites and introducing me to so many of the EM folks. I also want to thank my publishers, Jamie George and Frankie Howard-Gordon who have given so many hours of their time helping me to bring this book together. But most of all, I want to thank Glastonbury for being here when I needed Her.

Illustrations

Contents

Foreword

My interest in dowsing began in the U.S. in 1960 when my mother taught me how to dowse with wire coat-hangers using the pipe that brought water to our house as a target. I used my dowsing skills sporadically in the Sixties, and it really wasn't until the Summer Solstice in 1970 when she took me to see the Sunrise over some standing stones in central Vermont that I found a way to use dowsing in a meaningful way in my own life. On the evening before the Summer Solstice, about twenty of us gathered in Betty Sincerbeaux's house to hear dowser Terry Ross talk about things like ley lines, underground water and ancient power centers. Byron Dix, an archeoastronomer, was there as well telling us about the Summer Solstice Sunrise at Stonehenge and other examples of megalithic astronomy. It was fascinating!

Early the next morning, on the way to the astronomical platform, from which one could see the Sunrise on that day over a standing stone in a wall fifty yards to the northeast, I first came to a chamber of dry stone built into the side of a hill. It was covered with earth, and had a facade of stone with a door in the center. The stone chamber inside was ten feet by twenty. Seven massive lintel stones served as the ceiling, in the back of which was a shoebox-sized stone-lined hole, opening to the dawn sky above.

Terry briefly dowsed the chamber for Earth Energies, and then walked on to view the Solstice Sunrise from the nearby astronomical platform. I followed him and the others, but somehow, I found myself being drawn back to the chamber. As I had come for the Sunrise, I returned shortly to the platform, but soon found myself back in the chamber! Again, I rationalized myself back to the astronomical platform. But I was drawn back down to that chamber several more times, until I finally became resigned to the fact that I might not see the Sunrise that day.

Back I went into the chamber and sat down at the center of the back wall and looked out the front door. And then suddenly there were twenty-two other people there with me. These people hadn't come through the front door. They had simply just materialized. They were white, and some had beards; they had white togas on, and were sitting in a regular pattern cross-legged on the floor with their backs to the walls around the interior of the chamber. Three of them were sitting with their backs to the back wall, and I had the rather odd feeling that I was sitting in the same space as the one in the center. We were sharing the same space! I felt at peace, and literally at one with these "people".

Have you ever been meditating, and you suddenly become aware that you are having an especially good meditation? Then when you say to yourself, "Gosh a-rootie Buffalo Bob, isn't this great?", the answer is, "Not any more it isn't." When you become an observer, it's gone. That's what happened to me inside that chamber in Vermont. I said to myself something like, "Hey, this is really far out!" ("far out" was "in" back then) and they all disappeared.

I'm not even sure that the Sun ever came up that morning, but the essence of that experience has been with me ever since. Spiritual people from the past, using the extra power generated by the Solstice, and assisted by the energies of the place and its geometry, had broken through time to come to tell me in a most impressive manner that these chambers were important for my spiritual path. I had been with these "people" before, and they would help me now.

Since that Solstice, spiritual growth has been my goal, and dowsing has proved to be an invaluable tool to point the way. I have learned a great deal about sacred space, and the use of the Earth Energies, astronomy, sacred geometry, chanting, crystals, ceremony, and other things that enhance the possibility of heightened spiritual awareness. I have also found that healing is an integral part of this inquiry.

This is a book for fellow travellers on the spiritual path who would like to see if dowsing can help them along the way. With the resurgence of interest in dowsing, there has been an expanding awareness of its potential. Many new/very old ways of using these ancient tools are being re/discovered. Now there are people dowsing for all kinds of things from tangible targets like water, oil, treasure, lost objects and lost children, to intangible targets like the Earth Energies and the human aura. We are now finding that one can dowse for anything — the only limitations seem to be the dowser's imagination and level of consciousness.

As this book deals with the more spiritual aspects, we will focus on the intangible targets. This is a new concept for many people — looking for things one can't touch, taste, see, hear, or smell. Like the three blind men who were "looking" at the elephant, different Earth Energy dowsers often find different things at the same site. To the empirical scientific mind that operates in the world of repeatability, this is anathema. But, not to worry. Although there are some basic similarities that all dowsers should find, it is the differences that are so intriguing. These differences tell us each, as individuals, what we are ready to handle, what we are ready to know.

Dowsing then is a way of knowing. It's no good to just read about dowsing and not to experience it. This book is divided into two intermingling parts. The text gives you the intellectual food, and the exercises give you the practical experience.

The exercises will be in this kind of type.

This is a visual reminder to please try all of these exercises. Don't try to "do them in your head." It is the process of actually experiencing them that is important. In fact, if you are not willing to undertake the dowsing procedures suggested in this book, please read no further. You will just be wasting your time. You won't have the tools at the end to judge whether the material herein presented is relevant to you or not, whether or not it is a useful tool for you as a spiritual traveller.

This book is divided into three sections: 1. How to dowse, how to use the tools of the trade; 2. The Earth Energies, their possible use today, and a history of alignments of sacred spaces and secular monuments; and 3. Dowsing and healing. There are exercises and suggested further things to do throughout the book.

An important skill one needs to be a good spiritual dowser is balance. One has to have both a precise clearly defined picture of the target (objective), and an openess to the intuitive side from whence come the answers (subjective). An hypothesis of this book is that for the last two thousand years we have grown far too objective, analytical, linear thinking, patriarchal — out of balance. The term *Western Man* will refer to this kind of totally objective thinking and consciousness.

We need to be open to new ways for our Creator to move through us. We need to drop some of our outmoded ways of perceiving "reality". One way I've chosen to do this is to describe the time Before the Christian Era as *BCE*. The Christian Era itself is *CE*. These terms are less related to a specific religion than the more familiar AD and BC.

Some say there have been times when Matriarchs ruled large portions of this planet. Men were subservient to women. Then came the Patriarchs and women became subservient to men. It is a basic tenet of this work that neither of those modes is now acceptable. While the study of the Earth Energies is a study of polarities — night/day, female/male, Mother/Father, yin/yang — a balance of both is what is needed.

Even our language and grammar rules reflect today's male dominance and this lack of equality. The generic use of masculine-gender words often obscures or denies the contribution of women. In an attempt to make myself and you, dear reader, more aware of this lack of balance, I am using *s/he* instead of *he* and *wo/man* instead of *man* when the gender is not clearly male. Likewise, I use *her/his* and *her/him* instead of *his* or *him* when I mean *her or his/him*. If you notice that the use of these words irritates you, perhaps I have achieved my purpose. Take it as an indication of how far we have sunk into Western Man consciousness. To be a spiritual dowser, this needs to change.

While there is an initial emphasis here on the traditional dowsing tools, make no mistake. The ultimate goal of the spiritual dowser is to throw away the tools. While we begin with the Y rod and pendulum, we do so only as a way ultimately to turn on our *internal* pendulum and begin to experience the feeling of just knowing. Dowsing is a bridge leading you to worlds you never dreamed of — well actually, you've probably dreamed of them often. Once you've consciously crossed over that bridge, there's no turning back. I trust you will find that dowsing is a tool that can serve you well as a guide on the spiritual path.

— Sig Lonegren
March 1986

The Tools of the Trade

Dowsing: the word itself conjures up for most people visions ofold men holding forked sticks of apple wood looking for underground streams of water. The search for this precious liquid is certainly a part of this ancient art. Incidentally it was the only application of dowsing that was considered to be so valuable that it was allowed to survive relatively unscathed through the various persecutions of heretics and witches of the last thousand years. But as we now live in a time when Western Man — the rational mind and the scientific method — reigns supreme, beliefs and actions that were punishable by death only several hundred years ago are now tolerated; consequently, other kinds of dowsing are beginning to surface once again.

Today, dowsing is utilized in many different areas. Diviners are using their skills to locate off-shore oil, to find lost children, to diagnose illness, to study subtle energy fields like the human aura, and even to rediscover the energies of the Earth herself. It seems that the dowser is limited only by her/his imagination. You can dowse for anything you can imagine. More on this later. But first, what about the tools?

While the forked stick, or Y rod, is perhaps the best known of the basic dowsing tools, it is not the easiest tool with which to begin. There are actually four basic kinds of dowsing tools. In addition to the Y rod, L rods, as the name implies, are L-shaped rods held in the manner of Wild Bill Hickcock with his six-guns out ready to fire. The third dowsing tool is the bobber, something like a fishing pole held at the wrong end so that the heavier end can bob up and down or from side to side. But let's use the final dowsing tool, the pendulum, for your first practical experience.

In order for you to decide for yourself if dowsing actually works, you must try it. For this reason, it is absolutely essential that you provide yourself with a few simple tools. If you do not already own a pendulum, please dear reader, put this book down and get some thread and a ring, a metal nut, or any other similarly weighted small object. Tie the thread securely to the weighted object, and **voilà**! You have a pendulum. Please put the book down, and get/make a pendulum.

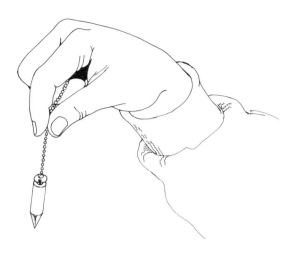

The Pendulum

Any balanced stable weight on the end of a string makes a pendulum, a tool that in its simplest application is good for asking "yes" or "no" questions. Hold the string between your thumb and forefinger, with the fingers pointing down. The length of string between your fingers and the weight depends on how heavy the weight is. The heavier the weight, the longer the string. You'll eventually discover what is the best and most comfortable for you. For now, try a length of three or four inches.

One of the most important notions that one encounters in dowsing is that each dowser must discover her/his own code. You need to identify three distinct and discreet responses in your pendulum: "search position", "yes", and "no".

The Search Position

The search position indicates a state of readiness from the pendulum's point of view. (We'll get into ideas about how it works later.) For some dowsers the search position is one in which the pendulum remains motionless. With others the pendulum oscillates back and forth.

You need to find out what your search position is, and you find this out for yourself. Sit down in a comfortable chair. Look at the pendulum with the expectation of seeing some pattern of movement. Again, hold the pendulum (fingers pointing downward) between your knees (a neutral area compared to directly over the right and left knees) and state, "Show me the search position." Feel which is better for you. What is your search position – stationary or back and forth? In either case, it says, "I'm ready. What's the question?"

Please try this now.

IF IT DIDN'T WORK. If your pendulum just hung there and did nothing, congratulations, your first dowsing experience was a total success! A motionless pendulum is your signal for the search position.

"Yes"

With that completely successful initial dowsing experience under your belt, let's try "yes". Not all dowsers have the same "yes" response.

Shift the position of the pendulum so that it is hanging directly over your right knee. Most dowsers find that the right knee is a source of yang (+) energy. How does your pendulum respond? For some, the pendulum indicates "yes" by oscillating back and forth, much as we nod our head up and down to indicate affirmation. For others, it goes from side to side, or rotates in either a clockwise or anticlockwise/widdershins (against the Sun) direction. It might even be something else.

With the pendulum over your right knee and in your search position, please find your "yes" response now by asking, "Show me 'yes'."

IF IT DIDN'T WORK THIS TIME EITHER. It's affirmation time! You can choose your "yes" response. The clockwise direction is used by many dowsers around the world as their signal for "yes", and is in resonance with many ancient traditions. So if your pendulum just hung there in what is your search position, teaching or programming it to move clockwise makes a good deal of sense. Dowsing is a tool that works for you. All you are setting up is the code.

Make the pendulum rotate in a clockwise direction. Say to yourself, "This is 'yes', this is yang, this is positive, this is clockwise, this is 'yes'." You may find that you have to make it go clockwise for several sessions; however, with persistence, it will ultimately seem to go by itself.

"No"

Now for the "no" response. Hold the pendulum over your left knee, and say, "Show me 'no'." (Notice which hand you're holding the pendulum in. Is it your left or is it your right? Whichever hand you've instinctively chosen, stay with it.) The left knee has been found to be a source of yin (–) energy on most people. From the search position, how does it move? Side to side? Anticlockwise? Some other way? As long as it is different from your "search" and "yes" positions, this is your "no" response.

IT STILL DOESN'T WORK! Have no fear. If you were interested enough to read this far, you can learn to dowse. Even though your first dowsing experience, the search position, was totally successful, not everyone always immediately gets a response for "yes" and "no". Learning anything takes time. If you want to be a good horseback rider, you're going to fall off. The important thing is that you get back up and try it again. Keep on trying. Practice is the key to success. This helps you to program these basic responses into your various levels of consciousness so that they all learn that specific motions of the pendulum have specific meanings.

Hold the pendulum between your knees. Notice the response. Say, "This is the search position." Then over the right knee (making it go clockwise if necessary), "This is my response for 'yes', it is yang, (+), positive, the Sun, it is 'yes'." Then over the left knee (making it go anticlockwise if necessary), "This is my signal for 'no'. It is yin, (–), receptive, the Moon, it is 'no'." Please try this now.

Do this exercise several times a day for one week, and the pendulum will be yours. Remember, only force the pendulum to move in a clockwise direction for "yes" and widdershins for "no" if you're not getting any action. Try this exercise again.

Sooner or later you will notice that your pendulum seems to be acting on its own. That's exactly what you want. After awhile, as you get into it, the various directions might change. If, all of a sudden, you're getting answers that don't make any sense, simply ask, "Show me 'yes'. Show me 'no'." While this doesn't happen very often, you could find that your signals have changed.

Tuning In

One of the major differences between a beginning dowser and a competent one is in her/his ability to tune in very specifically to the target. One way to start this focusing process is to try the following process whenever you begin a quest with your pendulum:

1. State what you want to do.
2. Ask, "Can I do it?"
3. "May I do it?"
4. "Am I ready to do it?"

First of all, you state what you want to dowse. Your pendulum will give you an affirmative to indicate that it understands. "Can" means do I have the dowsing skills? Am I capable of doing this? "May" talks about permission. Am I allowed to do this? While most kinds of dowsing hold no danger for the dowser, a few of the areas could get you into trouble if you get in over your head. One of these has to do with "ghosties and ghoulies and things that go bump in the night." So "May I?" is a useful question. And finally, "Is there anything that I may have forgotten? Am I sufficiently tuned in? Am I ready to go?"

You will be able to tune in to your subject or target much better if you use these four questions at the beginning of any dowsing exercise. On the other hand, if you use these questions, and you get a "no" on any of the four, stop. Something's wrong. If you go on anyway, you can't trust the answer. So why go on? Try the four questions over again rephrasing your initial statement more carefully and accurately. If you still get a "no", wait 'till later to try again.

Chakras

Now let's try some dowsing on a physical target. While our bodies have many chakras, or vortices of power (one pair is located in the knees, for example), we normally think of the seven that are aligned with our spines. Perhaps you have seen people from India who have a dot of color in the center of their forehead. This marks the third eye, or brow chakra. Christ refers to this center in Matthew 6:22 when he says, "The eye is the lamp of the body. So, if thine eye be single, your whole body will be full of light."

There are other chakras at the throat, the heart, and so on down the spine to the coccyx. But for this exercise, I'd like you to dowse the polarity of the crown chakra, which is found on the top of the head.

Find another human being – one who won't mind you dowsing around them. Once you have their permission, say something like, "I want to dowse the polarity of the crown chakra of this person. Can I? May I? Am I ready?" Assuming that you had all "yes" responses, hold your free hand just over the top of your friend's head. If your subject is a female, your pendulum will move into your yin, (–), "no" pattern. If it's a male, it will go into your yang, (+), "yes" response. Try it on another subject of the opposite sex. Notice the difference in swing. Please try this now.

Ask the person you are dowsing to move across the room. Point your free hand at their head, and ask to have an indication of the polarity of your friend's crown chakra. Notice your pendulum's reaction.

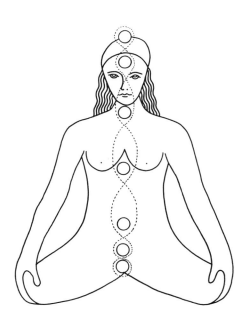

The Chakras

Map Dowsing

Now let's try the same exercise, but even one more step removed. Pick a picture of a man or a woman out of a magazine. "I want to dowse the polarity of the crown chakra of the person in this picture. Can I? May I? Am I ready?" Hold the fingertips of your free hand over their head. Once again, you will notice that your pendulum will define the yin or yang energy of that person even though s/he is in a photograph! (Note: if the person in the picture you are using is dead, you might get a different reaction either none at all, or the exact opposite of what you would expect i.e., a man's crown chakra, at the top of the head, reading yin or minus. Try asking, "Show me the polarity of this chakra at the time this picture was taken.")

This is called map dowsing, and all competent dowsers, no matter what their area of interest, employ this kind of dowsing to save themselves time in the field. Why walk all over forty acres of some farmer's land

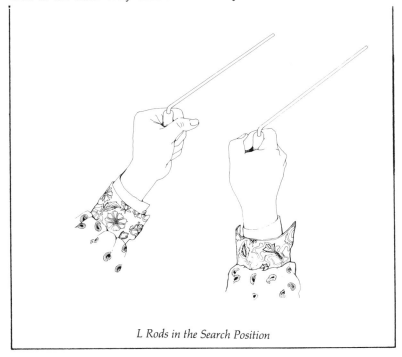

L Rods in the Search Position

looking for the best place to drill a water well when you can locate it rapidly and reasonably accurately on a hand-drawn map and then go out and quickly find and verify it in the field? It's not clear exactly how map dowsing works, but it does. And whether you are reading someone's crown chakra in a photograph, or looking for the best place to drill for water on a hand-drawn map, the process is still the same.

L Rods

As the name implies, L rods are L-shaped tools that are held by the shorter end of the L. They are usually used in pairs, one in each hand. These tools are most often made out of brazing rod, or other similar heavy-gauge wire. Some prefer to have sleeves on the shorter end so they can swing more easily. Beginners often make L rods out of two all-wire coat-hangers which are cut right next to the hook and at the other end of the bottom of the hanger. This bit can then be straightened out into an L. If you make a pair of L rods out of coat-hangers, you might want to bend over each of the ends of the wire to make sure that the rough ends don't injure anyone. While these coat-hanger L rods work reasonably well, the gauge of wire is light enough that out in the field the wind will blow them about more than you might like. This is why I prefer a heavier gauge of wire.

Let's try a different target for you to practice on with your L rods. Locate where the water-pipe enters your home (the main shut-off for your water is usually there). Then go outside and try to dowse for the pipe. Go to the point where you know that it leaves the house. Hold the L rods loosely in your hands with the longer ends of the wires pointing out in front of you – for me it has some of the feel of being a cowboy with my six-guns out and ready to shoot. This is the search position for L rods. Make sure that the longer end of the L isn't resting on your fingers. Say to yourself, "I am looking for the pipe that brings water into my home and I want the rods to cross when I get over that point." Walk confidently over your lawn with the expectation that your rods will cross.

If you have no idea where your water enters the house, put five or six feet of knitting yarn or string on your living room floor, and dowse for that instead (you can put it under the rug to make it a bit more authentic if you wish). The point here is to be dowsing for a known target. Please try at least one of these two exercises now.

THEY DIDN'T WORK. THEY DIDN'T CROSS! Sometimes beginners get intimidated by these new tools. It's important to remember that dowsing rods are tools that work for you — not the other way around. In this sense, they are a bit like animals that need to be trained. Try loving firmness. They're working for you. Show them what you want.

L Rods Crossing Over a Water-pipe

Once again approach the water-pipe or string with the L rods in the search position. When your hands are over the target, twist your thumbs toward each other. That's right, make the rods cross. What you are doing is impressing your subconscious how you want the rods to respond. You may have to do this six or seven times to make the connection. You may even have to do this for several days or even a week but, sooner or later, the L rods will begin to seem to be crossing by themselves. When you get this sense, continue to walk over your target paying more and more attention to the fact that you are in no way consciously moving those rods. When you can walk over the target, and know that you didn't twist your thumbs towards each other, then you are ready for the next step.

Go to a friend who wouldn't mind your dowsing around their house. With your L rods in the search position, walk around the outside of their home. State what you are looking for as clearly as you can. "I want my rods to cross over the pipe that carries the water into this house."

As you are walking, it is important that you keep a clear image of your target in mind and that you remain focused on that target. I use a **mantra** (of sorts). Mantras are sounds, phrases, or brief prayers repeated over and over again that help the spiritual seeker to keep focused. Perhaps the best known **mantra** is "Ommmmm". Another is done with the breath — breathing in, "My God", and exhaling, "My All". In the case of dowsing for a water-pipe, I would say over and over again with each step "water-pipe, water-pipe, water-pipe." This does not have to be said verbally, but that might help at first. It keeps you focused on the task at hand.

One of the major reasons for failure in dowsing is that between the asking of the question and the motion of the dowsing tool that indicates the answer, the dowser's need (conscious or unconscious) influences the answer. You will get what you want. As you are dowsing your friend's yard for the water-pipe, if you think to yourself, "it must be over there, where it's close to the main road," that's exactly where your rods will cross. You must not allow yourself to have expectations as a dowser. A *mantra* can help here as it not only keeps you focused, it also doesn't give you the time or opportunity to be thinking, "It must be over there."

When your rods cross, you can then go down into your friend's basement and see if you were right. If so, congratulations. If your rods crossed somewhere else other than where the water-pipe entered the house, perhaps they crossed over another pipe, maybe an older lead-pipe that used to bring the water in, or the pipe to the septic system. In any event, go outside again and pick up the water-pipe. You now know where it is. Feel that dowsing response. Can you think of any way to trace this pipe as it goes across the lawn or yard?

Again, if you are using yarn under a rug, have a friend hide a length under one of the rugs in your living room or a similar space. If you don't have rugs, use sheets of newspaper. Then you can use your L rods to look for the yarn in the same manner that you would look for a friend's water-pipe. When you have found the yarn, can you find out which direction it's running? This ability to trace the target is a skill that will come in handy later.

Up until now, your L rods have only crossed inwards. Stand near one of the water pipes or the piece of yarn, and say, "When I approach the target, I want my L rods to go out instead of in. When they are over the target, I want them to spread out so that when my hands are directly over the target, the arms of the L rods are spread out so that they are directly opposite each other." No matter what direction you approach the pipe or yarn from, you will find that when your L rods are directly over the target, the arms will oppose each other in such a way that you can tell in which direction the pipe or yarn is going!

There are times when you will want the L rods to cross in and other times when you'll want them to go out. The important issue here is they seem to be going "by themselves" and you are in no way consciously bending your wrists. Of course you can make the rods go either way by twisting your wrists, but who are you fooling?

The Y Rod

This is perhaps the best known of all the dowsing tools, and it is used by some of the hottest dowsers in the business. It is at its best when one is trying to pinpoint one specific target – a single point on the surface of the Earth. Before we discuss the forked stick in detail, it is important to remember that not all tools work equally well for all people. I found, for example, that after I had been dowsing for ten years or so, there was a period of two or three years when the Y rod didn't work for me. Without realizing it, I seemed to have convinced myself that the Y rod wouldn't work for me and indeed, it didn't. The L rods and pendulum worked fine, so it wasn't a big problem; however, in the late Seventies, when I was asked to head the Dowsing School with Ed Jastram for the American Society of Dowsers, I figured that it was time to get the Y rod to work for me again. So, I practised, and it came back. Need and intent are the critical factors here.

In dowsing, as in so many of the psycho/spiritual arts, need is very important. If you need to accomplish something — for example a friend doesn't have any water, and needs a well — dowsing works much better and more accurately than when you are showing off your dowsing skills at a party or in some trivial "scientific" experiment. I needed to have the Y rod work for me because I had to teach others ... so it worked. It really is as simple as that.

As a beginner, if you find that a certain tool doesn't seem to work for you, don't worry. Use the ones that do and improve your dowsing skills with them. When the time comes when you need to be able to use the one that hasn't worked for you, it *will* work. Don't worry about it.

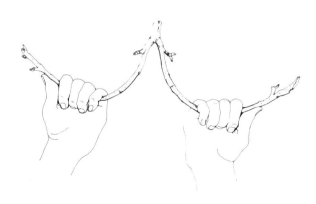

hands and Y rod

Back now to the Y rod. There is an old story that only certain woods will work for Y rods. In northern Vermont, where I come from, some dowsers swear by apple wood. In other areas, some feel that "only willow will work." My feeling about this is that if you believe that, it's true. On the other hand, if the ultimate goal of the spiritual dowser is to get rid of the tools entirely, what possible difference can it make what any given tool is made of? If you choose to limit yourself that way, you can do it. I feel that any Y-shaped material, be it apple wood, willow, white pine needles, or black plastic all work equally well as long as they are stiff enough and have a spring to them.

Before I cut a Y rod from a tree, I ask permission. This may seem odd to you at first, but if you want to learn how to tune in to Nature better, it's a good way to begin.

> Walk along looking for a Y-shaped branch with evenly-sized arms about the diameter of thick pencils. When you find a well-balanced branch, take out your pendulum and ask the tree if it is OK to cut that branch. (Remember: "This is what I want to do. Can I? May I? Am I ready?") When you get a "yes", say, "Thank you", and cut the branch. Trim off the excess twigs and leaves so that the two arms are about twelve to eighteen inches long.
>
> Grasp both arms of the Y rod with your palms upward, and your thumbs pointing out. The tip of the rod should be pointing upward (see illustration). You will find with a bit of maneuvering that there is a point of balance where if you were to move the stick just a bit forward, it would snap downward. Likewise, if you were to move it backward, it would snap you in the face! This "between the snaps" area is the Y rod's search position.

Animal

Now, what to look for. This time, let's try looking for underground water. Water dowsing is the one bit of divination that has survived those periods of time during which dowsers were actively persecuted by religious authorities. By some it's still called water-witching. Water is so important to life itself, but how to find it? Where to dig?

If we only had eyes to see, Mother Nature shows us clearly where veins of underground water are. This is true for the animal, vegetable and even mineral kingdoms. For example, cats love to spend time over crossings of underground veins of water. Do you have a cat? Is there someplace — not next to a heater — where your cat loves to sit? There could be veins of water there. If you have woodchucks (the American equivalent to the British badger) or foxes in your area, find the mouth of one of their tunnels or dens. These are always over a vein of water! Likewise ant hills are usually over a crossing of veins of water. Deer are very attracted to this elixir of life. Perhaps you can find a place in a pasture where they have bedded down for the night. The grass will be all matted down. This will also be over water. When bees leave a hive to go somewhere else, they first gather round their queen on the limb of a tree or some other object from which they can hang. This clump of bees is called a swarm, and it is always over underground veins of water.

Vegetable

If there aren't any of these animals in your area, maybe you can find a tree that has warty cancerous growths (in the U.S. we call these burls — good tobacco pipes are made from them). There will be a vein of water under that burl. Maybe you can find an apple tree in the middle of a pasture that, instead of growing straight upwards, leans out in an exaggerated way in one direction or another. It is stretching out to be over water. (At the edge of a wood, if you find a tree that leans out into the field, this is something else. It's called positive phototropism and it's just trying to get a bigger share of the sunlight.) Cedar trees lean out to grow over underground veins of water. There is an example of this in the Chalice Well Garden in Glastonbury, England. At the point where the tree turns upwards again, you will find a vein of water. Sometimes, when certain trees are rooted directly over a crossing of veins of water, the trunk twists like a corkscrew. I have noticed this with both apple and maple trees.

Mineral

If for some reason there are no cooperative plants or animals in your area, perhaps there is a megalithic standing stone, stone row, stone circle or other ancient sacred place. If someone hasn't moved the stones to "restore" them, they too will be over veins of underground water. Often there are two veins that cross directly underneath a standing stone, and they exit at the corners of the stone! The builders of these ancient sites must have been much cleverer than many scholars have realized.

In the sixth century C.E. Pope Gregory instructed his priests, who were then bringing Roman Christianity to the British Isles, to destroy the idols, but not the stones of the people, and to then build their churches on those same sites. This practice was continued by the Spaniards when they took over Central and South America. Most of their glorious cathedrals are built on Aztec, Mayan, Inca, etc. holy sites. But in the United States it was different. In their push westward, the settlers just wanted to get rid of the Indians. We wanted their land, so we tried our best to wipe them out. The European invasion of North America was probably the first invading culture that didn't find out where the indigenous people's holy sites were. Fortunately, Western Man wasn't totally successful in this venture and there are still some Native Americans who remember the old ways who are willing to share some of their knowledge with true seekers. There is more and more interest in these sacred places in the U.S. Ask around. When it is time for you to find one, it will be there. There is always water at these places.

Animal, Vegetable or Mineral, I'm sure that you can visualize at least one such place with an underground vein or veins of water near you. There are many ways Mother Nature speaks to those who will listen. These messages are found in the trees and plants, animals, and even in the mineral kingdom, in the Earth herself.

> Using the clues suggested above, find a place where animals, the vegetation or a standing stone shows that there is at least one vein of water under it. Ask with your pendulum, ("Can/May/ Ready?") "Is there a vein of water under this spot?" Then hold your Y rod in the search position, and say, "I want you to go down when I get over a vein of underground water." If possible, walk directly over the animal hole, crushed vegetation, or whatever your target is. You should feel a bit of a tug as you approach the target. When your hands are directly over the target, the stick should pull sharply downward.

IT DIDN'T WORK. I DIDN'T FEEL ANYTHING. It's time to train your dowsing muscles again.

> Walk over the target and **make** your Y rod go downwards. Say, "This is how I want you to react." It may feel odd to be talking to a stick of wood, but you need to program the expected response if it doesn't seem to work by itself. Walk over the target and make the stick go down several times. Then try it again with the expectation that it will work by itself. If it still doesn't work, and the L rods or pendulum did work for you, don't worry; put the Y rod aside for awhile, and concentrate on the tools that do work for you. (This is true for any of the dowsing tools. If one doesn't seem to work, use the others that do and come back to the

recalcitrant tool later.)

The Bobber

While some dowsers swear by this little device — especially oil and
water dowsers — the bobber is probably the least used of the four basic
dowsing tools. A good one can be made by holding a fishing rod at the
wrong end — by the tip. Hold the rod/bobber with either one or both
hands. Normally, the instrument will bob up and down to indicate
"yes", and it will go side to side to indicate "no". Using the same
method of "Show me 'yes' etc.", determine "yes" and "no" for you on
the bobber.

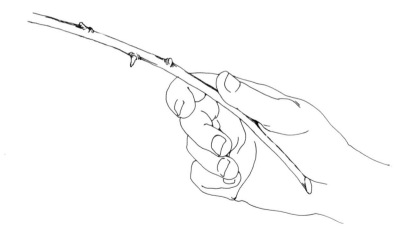

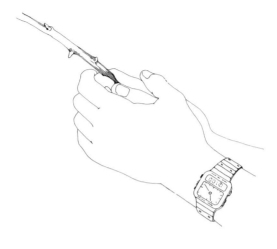

a bobber

This tool can also be used to determine the depth of the target. Stand over a vein of underground water. Tell the device that each bob will be ten feet and start counting the bobs. For example, if the top of the vein were fifty-four feet down, it would go something like this, "Ten, twenty, thirty, forty, fifty, sixty." At sixty, the bobber will start to move from side to side, so you know that it is more than fifty, and less than sixty feet down. Now change the code so that each bob represents only one foot. "Fifty-one, two, three, four, five." At fifty-five, the bobber will once again stop its bobbing and start to go from side to side, so you know that the top of the vein of water is between fifty-four and fifty-five feet down. You can take it to the nearest inch if you want to using the same process.

For me, the bobber goes up and down for "yes", and from side to side for "no", much like one moves one's head to indicate the same responses.

OK, I've Felt at Least One of These Tools Move
But
How Does It Work?

Unfortunately, there doesn't seem to be one simple answer to this question. Some have suggested that it works like radar; the dowser sends out some kind of searching signal and it bounces back. Others feel that target itself emits some sort of signal which the dowser picks up when s/he is directly over the target. Either certainly could be the explanation for how it works when an on-site dowser is directly over the target. Dr. Zaboj Harvalik, a past Trustee of the American Society of Dowsers (ASD) reported in their *Digest* that he could block the ability of his friend, Willie De Boor, to dowse veins of water that were directly underneath him by placing copper shields over the solar plexus and the head at the temples. (Why do you think that those two points on your head are called temples?) Dr. Harvalik felt that field dowsers picked up magnetic field gradients, his term for the dowsing signal, as they walked over the surface of the Earth looking for veins of water, underground pipes, mineral deposits or other specific underground physical targets.

This test would seem to indicate that with on-site, over-the-target dowsing, the signal can somehow be interfered with by shielding the field-dowsing sensors in the solar plexus and, to a lesser extent, those in the temple area of the head. So dowsing works like radar.

Not always. How would radar account for map dowsing? How does it explain the ability of most of the readers of this book to dowse the crown chakra of someone's picture in a magazine? How does radar account for "yes/no" dowsing when there is no physical target as such? It can't. The field-dowsing/radar model doesn't always work. Apparently, dowsing doesn't always work the same way. With an on-site dowser, it appears to work something like radar, but with map dowsing, and informational ("yes/no") kinds of work, there must be some other kind of explanation.

Holograms

Have you ever seen a hologram? If you have, you know that it has a remarkable ability to make two dimensions look like three. This effect is even more striking when the "object" you are looking at results from lasers being projected through a holographic negative. This negative doesn't look like an ordinary photographic negative of, say, an apple. A holographic negative looks like someone took a handful of pebbles and threw them at a pond. It looks like a series of circular radiating interference patterns.

If you were to take a regular photographic negative of an apple and tear a corner of it off and print just that corner, you would get just a bit of the apple. But with the holographic negative, if you tear off a corner and send coherent, or laser, light through it, you get the whole apple! The little corner has the whole within it. Granted, it won't be as crystal clear as the entire negative would have been, but the apple will still be there, in its entirety, hanging in space before your eyes.

Perhaps remote and informational dowsing works like that. Perhaps each of us, being part of the cosmic hologram, have the whole picture within us. We don't have to go outside of ourselves to get the answer. It already exists within.

The Seven Levels of Dowsing

Level One

Another way to look at the question of how dowsing works was developed by Terry Ross, past President of The American Society of Dowsers. I was fortunate enough to have him for one of my Field Faculty when I did my Masters Degree. He talks about seven levels of dowsing ability. His first, and lowest level of dowsing, is on-site dowsing, where the dowser must be directly over the target. This would equate with Dr. Harvalik's field dowsing and it probably does work something like radar.

Level Two

With level number two, the dowser can stand at the edge of the field and ask, "What is the direction of the nearest source of potable water that flows year 'round and is less than twenty feet under the ground?" With an L rod, hold one rod in the search position and turn your body. The L rod will "stick" in the direction where that water source is. With

a Y rod, again hold it in the search position, and turn slowly around in
a circle. When you're facing your target, the rod will dip, or go down.

> Try this with something near to you now like, "Where is the front
> door?" Holding your L rod or Y rod in the search position, turn
> slowly around in a circle. Notice that the rod seems to stick in that
> direction. The L rod will continue to point at the target even as
> you continue to turn, and the Y rod will dip as you pass that
> point. Obviously you know where the front door is, but this
> technique can be of benefit in many different situations. Can you
> think of a way to get your pendulum to indicate direction? With
> this second level, you're not over the target, but within sight of it,
> or at least close enough to walk to it. ("I'm lost in the woods,
> where's my car?")

Level Three

With level number three, the target is over the horizon. It is not within
your field of vision. It's a different way of going there; it's called map
dowsing. If you have been successful with all of the exercises in this
book so far, this is the level that you can now operate on. You did it
when you dowsed a photograph of someone to determine the polarity
of their crown chakra. Somehow, for the purpose of the search, the
symbol (in this case a photo) becomes reality. Many people who carry a
cross or a medicine bundle, or some other kind of spiritual protection,
don't feel that these objects are *symbols* of Christ, the Great Spirit or
whomever their amulet represents. Christ actually is there. The Great
Spirit is with them. The symbol *is* reality. They are one and the same.
Map dowsers work on that level.

Level Four

Level four is called "deviceless". You throw away the dowsing tool, and
just go inside and "know" the answer. Some people "see" a pendulum in
their mind's eye. They first see it in the search position and, after asking
the question, they see it move into their "yes" or "no" response. Why
don't you try this now?

> Say to yourself, "Can I do deviceless dowsing?" Relax. Take a few
> deep breaths and close your eyes. Look at the screen that you
> dream on. You'll find it in the center of your forehead, just above
> your eyebrows. (It's the place where you go when someone says,
> "Look at your mother" and you "see" a clear picture of her.) Now

go to that same place, and see your pendulum in your search position. See it move into your "yes" motion as it acknowledges your question and then it quickly goes back into your search position. "Can I do this?" "Yes." (At this point you already have your answer, don't you?) And so on. Give deviceless dowsing a try now.

IT DIDN'T WORK. I suspect that this might very well be the case for some of the readers. But please remember, fourth level dowsing is getting into some pretty rarified areas. There are many excellent old-time water dowsers who never go above level two. So if it didn't work, but map dowsing did, you're still in very good company. Keep at it; it will come.

Perhaps visually is not the way you might pick up level four information. With your eyes closed, try to picture your mother or a close friend. If you can't see the person, can you smell them? Feel their presence? Hear their voice? While the examples in this book for deviceless dowsing are mostly visual, if one of your other senses works better, use that one. "Hearing" the answer is as accurate as "seeing" it.

The holographic paradigm seems to be a good one to explain how levels three and four work. Some people call this information source the Akashic Record. In any event, perhaps we have this Great Cosmic Library within us. At these levels we have access to all kinds of information and, indeed, the first four levels are solely informational in nature. We are the recipients of answers to our questions that apparently come from a source other than our conscious rational mind.

Level Five

With level number five, things begin to change. At this level, healing seems to be a good example of what happens. Not only can the dowser go to another person and find out what the problem is — say lung cancer — but s/he can channel energy in such a way as to stop the cancerous growth. There are many examples of this throughout the dowsing community. And there is an important distinction here from the lower levels of dowsing. For the first time, the dowsers are not passive viewers. They can begin to effect someone or something outside themselves.

Spiritual House-cleaning

Another area where level five dowsing comes into play is with what dowsers refer to as "house-cleaning". While of course it is always beneficial to have your house cleaned on the physical level, this kind of cleaning has to do with spiritual levels of cleanliness. There are various types of energy that can make the environment of your home an unhealthy place to spend time in. Some people sense this immediately. Have you ever entered a house and just known that you wouldn't want to live there? You can't put your finger on exactly why, but it just doesn't feel right. There are several reasons why this might be so. The first one has to do with thought forms.

> Thought has form. To prove this to yourself, draw an imaginary line in the air with your finger. Pull out the dowsing tool you work best with, and ask it to find that line. When you come to the point in the air where you drew the line, your tool will react indicating the edge of that "imaginary" line! Try it.

Feelings and emotions also have form. When you have an angry scene with your mate, that energy continues to hang around, interfering with those who are trying to live in peace long after the angry scene. These forms can be erased. When I create intentional thought forms, after I'm through with them, I erase them by rubbing my hand over the form as if I were erasing a blackboard.

> Try this with the line you just created. Dowse it again to see that it is still there, and then erase it with your hand. As you do that, mentally make it your intent that the line be gone. Now dowse it again. See, it's gone! You can remove negative thought forms in the same manner from your home. It's all a matter of focusing your intent. You really don't need to do that rubbing action with your hand, but it helps you focus your intent.

Krebs Houses

In many homes, another kind of energy that negatively effects one's health comes from Mother Earth herself. Dowsers in Germany have known for years that there are certain houses where there is a much higher incidence of disease than in houses right next to them. This is true for family after family and generation after generation. They call these buildings krebs houses, the German word for cancer, because there is a particularly high incidence of that particular ailment in those homes. When dowsers were asked to look at these houses they found that there were a lot of veins of underground water crossing under them. The non-affected nearby houses didn't have this high incidence of veins of underground water. (Fault lines and mineral deposits are also sources of this kind of energy, but for the moment, let's stick to the water.) It is not actually the water itself that seems to cause the problem, although the flowing nature of the water seems to exaggerate it. The negative effect is more than twice as bad when one spends time over the crossing of several veins. Veins of flowing water seem to act as doors that allow certain energies to pass through the normally shielded mantle of the Earth's crust.

Muscle Testing

There is a way that you can feel this for yourself. It is called muscle testing or kinesiology. Your body can clearly tell you whether something is good for you or not. Find someone who will make a willing subject, and give the following a try. Locate a place where your dowsing rods tell you that there is a crossing of two or more underground veins of water. Once you have located them, ask the question, "Are these veins detrimental to human health?" (Some veins have been neutralized either by natural means or by the hand of wo/man. For this particular exercise, you must be working with veins that have not been neutralized.) Walk over the veins again. If you still get a dowsing reaction, continue with the test. If your rods remain in the search position, find another crossing of veins.

Have your friend stand near the crossing, but not over any vein of underground water. Tell her/him, "Hold out your right arm parallel to the ground." Put two fingers on the top of her/his wrist, and say, "I'm going to try to push your arm downward towards your waist, and I want you want you to resist." The technique is to say, "Resist", and then to exert the same downward pressure each time. Feel how much pressure it takes to move the arm downward towards her/his waist. Perhaps you won't be able to move her/his arm at all.

Now ask your friend to stand directly over the crossing of veins that you have previously dowsed as detrimental to human health. Try the same muscle testing exercise again, remembering how much pressure was necessary the first time. Your friend's arm will go down much more easily! This is a point on the surface of our Mother that will weaken us if we spend a lot of time over it.

Now comes the most important part of the test. Have your friend get off the crossing (back on to neutral turf) and test her/him a third time. You will find that her/his arm is strong again. Do not leave someone testing weak. Always make the last test a "strong" one. Have your friend try the same experiment with you, so you can **feel** how spots like these weaken you.

Incidentally, muscle testing can be used to test if certain foods or drugs are good for you. You might want to try the same procedure with sugar or tobacco. The person being tested can either hold the substance in their other hand, or they can put it on their tongue. It's a dynamite way to test for food allergies.

The Aura

Dowsing can also help you "see" the aura, that energy field that surrounds and permeates all living things. There are many ways of dividing up the human aura. Using inner vision, a form of deviceless dowsing, some see the health aura as a glowing band of shimmering colors extending about six to eight inches from the body. This band of color is a statement about the person's health and mental attitude. In addition to the health aura, others see an egg-shaped spheroid field extending many feet outwards.

As a dowser, I have found that the aura can be divided vibrationally into seven bodies starting with the lowest vibrational one, our physical body, and expanding outwards to the point where our seventh, or highest vibrational body, covers the entire cosmos. It is at that level that we are one with the Creator.

Obviously then, the outer edges of some of these bodies can not be dowsed here on Earth. But we can dowse the first three or four. The lowest vibrating body is the Physical. It can be experienced empirically. You can touch it with your finger. The first one beyond the Physical, and the one we shall use for this dowsing experiment, is called the Astral or Emotional body. It vibrates at a higher rate than our Physical body which it interpenetrates, and it extends some two or three feet out from the Physical body. Usually when I ask to dowse the edge of someone's Astral body, when I find it, and extend my arm out and touch their chest, the edge is somewhere between my elbow and my chest. The Astral/Emotional body will be the body that we will practice with. The next body out is the Mental body, and beyond that, the Spiritual. (See the Sevens Chart at the end of this chapter.)

For the next dowsing exercise you need a willing subject. I can't stress how important that word "willing" is. You must have the person's permission before you dowse for information about them. There are always some unaware sods at dowsing conventions who insist on jabbing their Y rods into people's auras without asking permission.

When it has happened to me, it feels like an invasion of privacy. And that's just what it is. You wouldn't go into someone's house without asking permission, so why go into their psychic space without doing the same?

> In any event, ask your friend to stand at a point where you have determined that there are no underground veins of water. Dowse the edge of their Astral body. Notice where that edge is on your outstretched arm when you touch their chest.
>
> Then ask your friend to stand over the spot where you have previously determined through dowsing and muscle testing that there is a crossing of underground veins detrimental to human health. Dowse the edge of the Astral or Emotional body again. Notice that it has shrunk to within several inches of the physical body. Then ask her/him to go back to the neutral space and notice how the aura expands again.
>
> For me, this is evidence of psychic attack. If you were to walk naked outside into a winter storm, your body would go immediately into a series of contractions – shivering. The same is true on the higher levels of our auric bodies as well.

Level Six

The sixth and seventh levels of dowsing are rarified indeed. The sixth level dowser can not only go there and, say, halt the cancer in the lung, but s/he can can be a channel for healing energies that will create new lung tissue in place of the old. It's one of those times when the doctor looking at before and after x-rays of a patient's lungs has trouble thinking it's the same person.

Level Seven

With the seventh level, the dowser and their Creator are One. "Thy will be done." And it is. Christ and the other Avatars function on this level. It is the highest level that one can operate on and still be in the physical body.

So the dowser seems to grow from level to level. As s/he completes one s/he is ready for the next. It begins with on-site dowsing. Level two is where the dowser takes the first step away from having to be directly on top of the target to being able to dowse from the edge of the field. The third and fourth levels take the dowser further and further away – first map dowsing, then doing away with the tools entirely. Fifth level dowsers can go someplace and change things — stop a cancer, move a vein. At the sixth level, new material can be created. The seventh, and highest level is called reflexive. The dowser's will and the Great Spirit's will are one.

Dowsing Skill Levels	Chakra Number	Chakra Polarity to Hyp. (F M)	Name	Notes	Element	Our Seven Bodies		Color	Tom Graves' Standing Stones / Energy Release Points
Reflexive~ ..one...	7	− +	Crown	B	Spirit [cardinal]	Divine	Higher Bodies	Orchid	Very occasionally acts directly on spine muscles of dowser, producing a violent electric-shock-like reaction.
Creative~ "Go there" and create things	6	+ −	Brow	A	Thought [mutable]	Monadic		Purple	No direct action on dowser; but "transmits" as long-distance straight line overground communications
Alteration~ "Go there" and change things	5	− +	Throat	G	Ether [fixed] (sound)	Causal		Blue	Acts directly on dowser's balance, thrusting dowser to left or right; direction of apparent thrust changes 6th day after new & full moon
Deviceless dowsing~ can "visit" target. Informational	4	+ −	Heart	F	Air (touch)	Spiritual/ Intuitional	Psyche/Soul	Green	No direct action on dowser; but transmits short-distance ("internal") stone-to-stone/straight-line overground communications
Map Dowsing	3	− +	Solar (Navel)	E	Fire (sight)	Mental		yellow	No direct action on dowser. Ground Level
Remote Dowsing (at edge of field)	2	+ −	Spleen (sacral)	D	Water (taste)	Astral/ Emotional	Lower Body	Orange	No direct action on dowser
Field Dowsing~ Directly over/on target	1	− +	Root	C	Earth (smell)	Etheric / Physical		Red	No direct action on dowser
Terry Ross	•	Graves	Leadbeater		Rendel	Tansley		Color Healing	Ley Hunter #79 ←Sources

* The Sevens Chart

Dowsing the Earth Energies

Dowsing is best known as a tool for locating underground veins of water, oil, lost objects, missing persons and buried treasure. Note — these are all physical targets. This kind of dowsing yields itself easily to evaluation by the scientific method. When the forked stick goes down, the target is either there, or it isn't. Physical-target dowsers' work can be checked by observation, by digging or drilling.

On the other hand, when one is intent on using dowsing as a tool for spiritual growth, the process isn't quite so easy. How can one "prove" that one has found an edge of the human aura (a field of energy found around all living things) when there are presently no scientifically acceptable tools to measure it? (Isn't it interesting that some have given machines the power to define reality?) True to his veneration of analytical, linear thinking, twentieth century Western Man has determined that something is real only if he can see, smell, hear, taste, feel it. Or if a needle moves on a machine. What a limiting and limited view of reality!

At sacred centers, a dowser finds all kinds of Earth Energies, s/he can feel them as well, but as yet, they certainly haven't been demonstrated empirically. How can someone scientifically demonstrate that they have grown spiritually? And yet most of you who are reading this *know* that in the last several years you have grown at least a bit closer to your Creator. This is an awareness that all on the path have. And yet, how can that be proven scientifically? It can't. While physical-target dowsing can be proved empirically, intangible-target dowsing, spiritual dowsing, isn't as easily verified by the scientific mind-set.

Western Man has based his primacy on logical thought and the five senses. Auras and Earth Energies — in fact all the intangible targets of the spiritual realms — don't yield themselves easily to this method of viewing reality. Dowsing can help us begin to look into those worlds beyond the five senses. It is a bridge that can help us touch the intangible.

Primary Water

Dowsing is a tool we can use to help us "see" the Earth Energies at sacred sites. Every valid site that marks a ley line, an alignment of sacred sites, has water under it. There are two kinds of underground water. There is the "water table" water that most hydrologists are interested in. The other is "primary water" (some call it "juvenile water"). Primary water doesn't come from rain water, but rather is created in the bowels of the Earth as the by-product of various chemical reactions. This water is then forced under pressure towards the surface of the Earth in what dowsers in the United States call "domes" (in Great Britain, they are called "blind springs"). I picture domes to be like geysers that just don't reach the surface. The water continues its upward journey until it hits an impermeable layer of rock or clay. The pressure then forces the water out horizontally, in what dowsers call veins — cracks and fissures in the rock. As a spiritual dowser, one can find domes or crossing veins of primary water under any valid marker of a ley line. When these veins of primary water reach the surface in many parts of the world, they are considered to be holy wells, places of healing and spiritual contemplation, places of the Earth Mother.

An Agreement on Primary Water

There is one aspect of the Earth Energies that as dowsers we should all be able to agree on. This has to do with the presence of primary water at these sites. It's always there. For this reason, if you want to become a good Earth Energy dowser, I urge you to work — at some time in your development — with a competent drinking-water dowser. Apprentice yourself to one long enough to be sure that where s/he finds water, you find water. This sure knowledge of the location of underground veins of water is critical in determining not only how the veins dance at power centers, but where there are zones in a home that are detrimental to a person's health. A spiritual dowser must also be a water-witch.

In the nineteen-thirties, Reginald Allender Smith was one of the first dowsers to write about finding water as a primary ingredient of any sacred space. This has been corroborated by many fine dowsers since his time. I have worked with Bill Lewis, one of the master dowsers of the British Isles; Tom Graves, author of several important books on dowsing and the Earth Mysteries; and Terry Ross, the person who brought the notion of dowseable leys to the United States. All of them find primary water under valid markers of the ley system. I believe it is time for all Earth Energy dowsers to agree on this. It is always there. Too many good dowsers have been finding it for too long now for it not to be there. If you are not finding primary water at sacred sites, once again, perhaps it is time for you to go spend time with a water-well dowser.

Ley Lines and Energy Leys

Ley lines, these alignments of sacred sites, are the result of our ancestors locating their holy sites over primary water. Dowsers have found that many, but by no means all, of these ley lines also have straight beams of male, or yang, energy flowing along them. These are called "energy leys". Energy leys are normally six to eight feet wide, and have a direction of flow, like a river. In England, most ley lines (but again, not all) have these energy leys flowing concurrently with them. In New England where I did my Masters research, I know of four or five ley lines, but I have dowsed well over four hundred energy leys.

Sacred Space

This Earth of ours (the Greeks called her Gaia) has always had a series of places all over her surface where the yin and the yang, the female and male, the domes and veins of primary water and the straight energy leys have come together forming what is called a "power center". The energies at any given power center (defined as a minimum of one vein of primary water crossed by one energy ley) are not always the same throughout the year. Each one reaches its peak of power at one or more times during the year based on various factors including what the Sun, Moon, and to a lesser extent, other stars are doing. When an energy ley aligns with the rising or setting of the Sun, for example, the ley becomes much more potent.

Many temples and other sacred spaces are associated with specific times of the year — Stonehenge with the Summer Solstice Sunrise, Newgrange with the Winter Solstice Sunrise, Solomon's Temple with the Equinox Sunrise. At these times, the energy ley that runs along the site's major axis joins the power center there with the point on the horizon where Sun rises or sets on that Solstice, Equinox, or Cross Quarter day. (If you think of the Solstices and Equinoxes as dividing the year up into quarters, the Cross Quarter days divide the year up into eighths, and occur at the beginnings of November, February, May and August.) Other sites are oriented towards the rising points of the Moon, Venus, or certain stars. In these cases, the point on the horizon marks a significant place in the cycle of that particular heavenly body. Whatever the alignment, it creates a massive increase in the energy available at that particular power center at that particular time. Different sites were set up to utilize this energy in different ways. So different sites used their major axis astronomical alignment to enhance the intent of the builders to use these energies for healing, for fortelling the future (the veil to the other side being thinner at that point), for fertility (the priests of the Nile were responsible for the fertility of that ancient valley), or for general growth in spiritual consciousness.

His Story and Her Story of Alignments

Until the discovery of the Nag Hammadi documents just after World War II, the only thing we knew about Gnostics, an early Christian sect who were judged to be heretics, was what was written about them by the early Church Fathers who didn't like them. Most of what we know about Feng Shui, Chinese geomancy, comes from Ernest J. Eitel, a Christian missionary to China who, once again, didn't like this heathen practice. History is written by the victors. The patriarchs. But what about herstory? One of the things that I remember from somewhere in my training to become a Western Man was the notion that there is no such thing as a straight line in nature, and yet, since the beginning of recorded time, we humans have known and utilized the power of alignment. From the alignment of passage graves and standing stones constructed in the middle of the fourth millenium Before the Christian Era (BCE) to the present day intentional alignment in Washington, D.C. of the Lincoln Memorial, the Tidal Basin Pool, and the dome of the rotunda over the Capitol of the United States, we humans have been using alignments. Prior to the dawning of Western Man consciousness, these alignments were used for spiritual purposes, to mark centers of, among other things, healing, fertility and prophesy. This kind of alignment, a ley line, might consist of holy sites from many different periods throughout history.

Until roughly the time of the Protestant Reformation, the people of Europe built their sacred sites in straight lines, ley lines, that ran across the countryside in harmony with the Earth Energies. Since that time, Western Man has continued to use the power inherent in alignments, but for different purposes. Let us look then at our use of alignments throughout herstory and history to see how we might use dowsing as a spiritual tool.

Until the beginning of the Neolithic (New Stone Age) period, roughly 4000 BCE, Europeans were hunter-gatherers. As we followed the herds and the various crops that ripened in their time, we were in tune with Nature, and were naturally at the appropriate power centers at the specific time of the year we needed to be there to perform our various ceremonies and rituals. Gaia led us to the right place at the right time, and our spiritual lives prospered accordingly. John Michell has a good discussion of this concept in his book, *Earth Spirit*.

The First Farmers

When we settled down and became farmers however, we had a problem — we had to make do year 'round with the power centers that were in our local area. We then had to find ways to enhance the Earth Energies at times when they were not at their peak. The archeological evidence indicates that by the middle of the Neolithic period we were building incredibly sophisticated sacred enclosures that, among other things, demonstrate a thorough knowledge of geometry thousands of years before the Greeks supposedly invented it! These sacred sites were built on previously existing Earth Energy power centers, utilized sacred geometrical ratios in their construction to enhance the energy, and were oriented towards specific horizonal astronomical events. All of this was done, apparently with an incredible amount of human labor, to know better when the energies would reach their zenith and, at other times of the year when they were at lower levels of intensity, to concentrate them for use in spiritual activities. There seems to be a solid connection between the introduction of farming and our first permanent temples built on sacred space.

The Earliest Alignments

The earliest use of alignments that I know of is found in Ireland. In the lush green valley of the Boyne River north of Dublin, Neolithic people of about 3500 BCE created a spectacular array of massive circular mounds of earth with cruciform stone-lined tunnels called passage graves. Some align with the Sun as it rises and sets at significant points of the year — Solstices, Equinoxes and Cross Quarter days. Others line-up with similar structures, standing stones and smaller burial mounds that resemble round barrows.

Martin Brennan has done some magnificent work with these Irish passage graves and has identified the oldest ley lines that I know of in the world. A good example would be the alignment that starts at Knowth, a passage grave with two stone-lined tunnels, one oriented to the Equinox Sunrise, and the other to the Equinox Sunset. About three quarters of a mile to the southeast, the line runs through a standing stone, one of a dozen that surround the best known passage grave of all, Newgrange. The cruciform chamber of Newgrange is oriented towards the Winter Solstice Sunrise. The line from Knowth goes through that chamber where the main tunnel and side chambers converge. (Many other alignments with other sites and/or astronomical events also cross at this point as well.) The alignment then exits the passage grave and goes through another of those twelve stones that surround the site. The alignment ends about a half a mile further to the southeast where it hits Mound 6, one of the round barrow-shaped mounds that are also found in the valley of the Boyne River. Five points within two miles, all are related to ritual, and they're in a straight line.

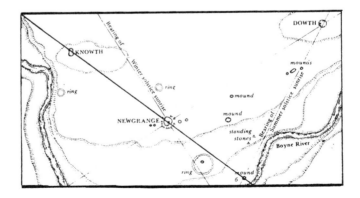

(From Brennan's Book Boyne Valley Vision. P. 28)

The Boyne Valley

Several hundred years after the construction of the Boyne Valley complex, the Neolithic people of south-central England constructed an enormous sacred megalithic complex, a landscape temple that truly staggers the mind. She is called Avebury.

Avebury

Ah Avebury! One's being is confounded and delighted by the impressive West Kennet long barrow, a magnificent burial chamber oriented towards the Equinox Sunrise, and Silbury Hill, the largest wo/man made prehistoric mound in Great Britain (in all of Europe, for that matter). And then there is the magnificent henge monument itself, the Avebury stone circles. There are three of them, two small (or should I say normal-sized circles) inside the truly enormous ring of huge sarcen stones. These megaliths delineate and dominate the inner bank of the deep ditch and towering outer bank that create the henge. All of this was accomplished around the beginning of the third millenium before the Christian era by Stone Age farmers using antlers for picks and oxen hip-bones for shovels.

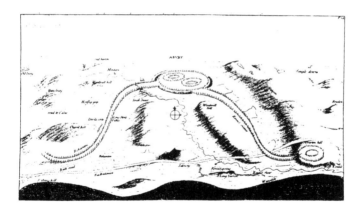

William Stukeley's Map of Avebury

But let's turn our attention to that apparently serpentine West Kennet Avenue. It consists of two rows of large, mostly either diamond- or phallic-shaped stones that run parallel to each other for over a mile and a half from the the circles at Avebury to a smaller circle of stone and wood posts called the Sanctuary, located above the hamlet of East Kennet. In the eighteenth century drawings of Avebury by William Stukeley, the West Kennet Avenue is one of two that run from outlying sites to the main circle, much like the fallopian tubes go to the uterus in the human female reproductive system. Following this logic, the Sanctuary would be analogous to one of the ovaries. Perhaps this image stretches things a bit, but make no mistake; we are in the territory of the Earth Mother.

It turns out that rather than being serpentine, seemingly constructed in a series of arcs, the West Kennet Avenue is actually made up of a series of straight lines. Paul Devereux, Director of the Dragon Project, and I have been interested in the alignment potential there for some time. At the top of the first gradual rise leading away from the henge itself is one particular segment of that series. It includes two of the larger stones that are left in the entire Avenue. Their major axes align along one of the best ley lines I have ever seen. These two stones are aligned in such a way that one can just see between them. In one direction — to the southeast — one sees the tip of another standing stone in that row and above it, a round barrow in the distance can be seen through the slit between the two stones.

To the northwest, in the opposite direction, the steeple of the village church in Avebury can be seen through the vesica pisces frame of the stones in the Avenue. In the mid-ground between the church and the sighting sarcen stones, the ley runs along a perfectly straight section of the massive ditch of the Avebury henge itself. This occurrence of a ley line tangentially striking circular prehistoric features is quite common in Britain.

Avebury Four-inch Wide Ley Line – to the Southeast

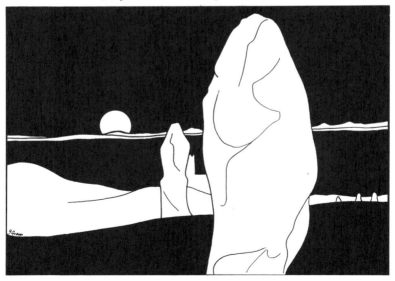

Avebury Four-inch Wide Ley Line – to the Northeast

So here we have an alignment that has six valid points on a dead straight line in less than a mile and a half! On top of that, the two stones in the middle of the ley focus one's vision to an incredibly narrow visual alignment in both directions. The points all have primary water under them. It's the tightest ley line I've ever seen. It's about four inches wide! While there is primary water under each of the points, there is no dowseable energy ley running concurrently with that ley line.

This seems to be a second phase in our ancestors' use of alignments. The first ley lines developed naturally as a result of building on power centers. There was no intent to put the sites in a line; it just happened because some of the sites were on the the same energy ley. But by the time of the construction of the West Kennet Avenue, we had learned how to make intentional alignments that didn't necessarily have energy leys flowing along them. Still, the specific points were chosen because they had primary water under them.

Stone rings like Avebury have been found to mark the crossings of two or more ley lines. Dowsers find that they also mark the crossing of energy leys over primary water. One of the ongoing spiritual aspects associated with ancient sacred sites is fertility. Perhaps those who worked with the Earth Energies might have wanted to spread their fertilizing aspects over more of the countryside. (Being a country boy, a vision of a spiritual manure spreader comes to mind here.) Having realized that the holy places were naturally aligning themselves, perhaps these non-energy ley lines might have served as channels for energies of fertility that were reflected down them from power centers like Avebury.

Tom Graves' Cyclotron On the Avebury Four-inch Ley

A cyclotron is used by physicists to speed up atomic and sub-atomic particles in a circular accelerator by spinning them round and round until they reach the appropriate velocity. The particles are then shunted off on to the target. Dowser Tom Graves has suggested a cyclotron effect at Rollright stone circle. Graves found energy being spun around the circle, and then released outwards at various points along the circumference. This cyclotron effect is especially interesting when we consider our Avebury non-energy ley line is tangent to the circle. The only non-Neolithic point on that ley is the Christian church, and, as one of the points, it stands alone to the northwest of the circle, on the wrong side of the flow. All the other points are to the southeast. If the energy at the Avebury circle were swirling in a widdershins or counterclockwise direction, and released at the point where our non-energy ley line is tangent to that circle, it would flow down that ley, along the Avenue towards the round barrow on the horizon, thus spreading the fertilizing potential of these power centers.

All of the ley line markers discussed at Newgrange and at Avebury (standing stones, passage graves, round barrows, the henge monument and the church) have primary water under them. All except for one — the church at Avebury — were built or constructed at least two thousand years before Christ, and many of them three thousand BCE. All of them have clear unambiguous connections with ritual, ceremony and sacred space. The first ley lines were the unintentional result of early farmers working with their local power centers to access the source of spiritual power on a year 'round basis. The alignments just happened. They were the result of putting ceremonial sites on places where the yin comes together with the yang, where Earth Mother comes together with the Solar Father. Within five hundred years of the earliest leys, by the first part of the third millenium BCE, wo/man had learned to construct intentional alignments that connected sacred sites, but did not necessarily run concurrently with energy leys.

It is difficult to find strictly Neolithic ley lines. There are some good examples in Cornwall, and at the Devil's Arrows up in Yorkshire, but people all around the world have been intentionally building their sacred sites on power centers until comparatively recent times. Europeans did so until around the end of the time of the great Gothic Cathedrals. Some people, the Aborigines of Australia, geomancers in Hong Kong, and some Native Americans, just to mention a few, are still doing it today. As a result of this multiple cultural use of the same Earth Energy system, ley lines tend to be somewhat mixed in the sense that there are sacred sites of quite different time periods on the same alignment. This is a particularly hard one for archeologists and anthropologists to understand because they just can't imagine that something that we don't know about today was recognized by those primitive savages, utilized by various succeeding pagan cultures, and also known by those men of God who built the Gothic Cathedrals. We forgot because the witch trials and other heresy persecutions of Western Man made us forget. But more of that later.

The First Signs of Western Man

At about one thousand BCE one finds a new feature intruding into the confines of what initially had been sacred alignments. Bit by bit, the secular begins to intrude. John Barnatt, an archeologist who has done a lot of work on Dartmoor and up in the Arbor Low area in Derbyshire, has postulated that the archeological evidence seems to suggest that prior to around the second millenium before Christ, the people were held together (perhaps controlled?) by spiritual power — healing, fertility, oracular, and heightened awareness. Everyone experienced this power. The ceremonial centers starting with a big blast at Avebury in the fourth millenium were followed by the builders of the magnificent stone rings. These became more and more complicated until they culminated with the magnificent sarcen trilithons of what is called Stonehenge III in about fifteen hundred BCE. It was as if we were building more and more elaborate structures to hold down that elusive quicksilver energy. And we were forgetting how to do it.

At Stonehenge, we can see this shift in a different way. Stonehenge was constructed in three different chunks. Stonehenge I was the earliest, 2600 BCE ± and consists of the henge (the ditch and bank), the four small Station Stones that dot the Aubrey Holes (52 circular chalk-filled pits just inside the ditch), and the Heel Stone(s). Everyone could clearly see what was going on at the center. Everyone could be involved.

Stonehenge II added the human-sized Prescelly Blue Stones around 2000 BCE. When the builders of Stonehenge III in the middle of the second millenium BCE added the tall trilithons in the center, the lay people around the periphery could no longer see what was going on in the center. A similar development took place in the development of rood screens in the Gothic Cathedrals 2500 years later. Perhaps this represents a move on the part of the priesthood to consolidate their power. In any event, the end result of the trilithons and rood screens was that less

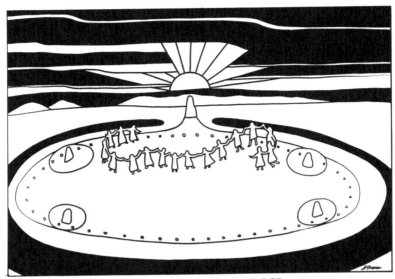

Ceremony at Stonehenge I, 2600 BCE

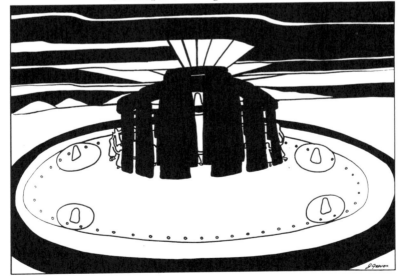

Ceremony at Stonehenge III, 1500 BCE

and less people really knew what was going on. This concentration of spiritual power into the hands of a few led next to the desire to have power down on the physical level as well. And there's good evidence for this in the Iron Age that arose just after Stonehenge III, around 1000 BCE.

There's a famous ley line that Sir Norman Lockyer, an early astroarchaeologist/archeoastronomer (interested in astronomy and how it relates to ancient sites), found at the turn of this century. It begins at a tumulus (2000 BCE ±) just north of Stonehenge where it runs tangentially to the circular ditch (2600 BCE ±) and then on to an Iron Age hill fort called Old Sarum. Hillforts were an introduction of the Iron Age which began in southern Britain at around 1000 BCE. They were defensive military positions, the first points on leys that were clearly not ritualistic in nature. Two millenium later, the Normans put a military camp in the center of this hill fort. Shortly thereafter, an impressive church was also built at Old Sarum; however, the soldiers and the priests didn't get along, so someone fired an arrow into the air, and the present Salisbury Cathedral was constructed where it landed. The ley line does not go through the spire of that building which towers over the crossing of the knave and transcept, but rather, it goes through the high altar, to the east of the spire. The ley line then continues through two further Iron Age hill forts, Clearbury Ring and Frankenbury Camp.

Stonehenge/Old Sarum/Salisbury Cathedral Ley
After Norman Lockyer

It is with the inclusion of hill forts in the Iron Age, all of which still have primary water under them where the ley strikes them (many times only a glancing blow), that the use and function of ley lines in Britain begin to change. As Barnatt points out, the people weren't being controlled and ruled by the spirit any more, but by force. Hill forts were not sacred places; they were one man's, a family's, or clan's statement to the world about their physical power.

The Romans

The Romans carried on this use of leys for physical purposes when they built their famous roads on the more ancient ley lines. The Romans have always been praised for their roads. The reality is that they built only the surface of them. These straight tracks had been used for millennia as sacred ways, but the Romans debased them by using them as ways of quickly getting their armies around Europe. They used spiritual paths for military purposes. Actually, except for the many examples of Roman roads on ley lines, there are very few other Roman structures in England that are on these alignments. With a few exceptions, like the foundations of Wells Cathedral, the Romans just didn't seem to build many other structures on ley lines here in Britain. The Romans were the first people to use these sacred ways for secular purposes as a matter of national policy. But they weren't the last. Throughout the rest of history there is more and more evidence for secular use of alignments.

Pope Gregory and the Benedictines

In the sixth century CE Pope Gregory, in a letter to those who were to carry Catholicism to Britain, cautioned these missionaries not to destroy the ancient sites. Gregory wanted them to destroy the idols, for sure, but he urged them to build churches on the older holy places. Even if these missionaries did not know of these Earth Energies (some clearly did as evidenced by some beautiful Medieval ley lines) their churches would therefore have been automatically linked to the alignment of earlier holy sites. Again, just by choosing to place his churches on the previous culture's sacred spaces, Gregory assured that they fell into straight lines as they dotted the countryside of Dark Age Britain.

At least part of the Church at that time, the Benedictines, were well aware of these Energies. In fact Gregory was a Benedictine himself! The Order was founded by St. Benedict in the first half of the sixth century CE. Unlike earlier orders of the Church, the Benedictines stressed communal living, and their abbeys were like homes of Christian families with abbots as fathers. Perhaps the most fascinating aspect about them is that throughout Europe, these Benedictine abbeys and monasteries were built on major power centers — sites with much earlier spiritual connections as well. Monte Cassino in Italy is one. And so is Monserrat, a major pilgrimage site on the side of a mountain of the same name northwest of Barcelona in Spain where there is also a black wooden image of the Virgin supposedly carved by St. Luke. Monserrat was thought to have been the castle of the Holy Grail. At Fulda, in Germany,

St. Boniface founded a Benedictine abbey. It was from Fulda that Christianity spread throughout central Germany.

The St. Michael's Geomantic Corridor

In the English Channel there are two well-known island power centers that utilized the ley system for sacred purposes. Both are islands at high tide only; at low tide they both connect with the mainland. Both Mont St. Michel off the coast of France and St. Michael's Mount off the coast of Cornwall in southwestern England were Benedictine abbeys. St. Michael's Mount is at one end of an infamous geomantic corridor or dragon path that runs in a northeasterly direction to the Beltane (May Day) Sunrise. It runs through a series of important English power centers including many that are dedicated to St. Michael or to other dragon-killing saints like St. George and St. Margaret. It traverses England from St. Michael's Mount to at least as far as the St. Michael's church in Clifton Hampden, almost two hundred miles to the northeast in Wiltshire. Because of its length, there is a great deal of controversy as to the relative straightness of the entire line. Part of the problem is that due to the curvature of the earth, one should be employing spherical geometry rather than plane geometry to calculate its straightness.

Three of the points in the middle of this geomantic corridor are of particular interest. The southern entrance of Avebury is at one end, and Burrow Bridge Mump in Somerset is at the other. The major axis of the Mump (mound) aligns with this corridor. In between them is perhaps the most famous of the St. Michael points on this dragon path – the Glastonbury Tor, whose major axis also runs along the May Day (Beltane) alignment. Glastonbury was an island at the time when Joseph of Arimathea, the uncle of Jesus, came and built the first above ground Christian church shortly after the crucifixion. The Celtic Christianity that was formed was a beautiful blend of Christianity and Druidism; the Christ energy was an important source when working in the spiritual realms, but Nature was also held in reverence. Glastonbury remained an important Celtic Christian shrine until it was taken over in the 10th Century by guess who? – the Benedictines. It then became one of the most powerful religious centers in England until Henry VIII broke it up in 1539.

By holding the important mountains and other geomantically strategic sites, the Benedictines attempted to control Europe for the Church. As they built on power centers, their monasteries and abbeys were automatically plugged-in to the ley line system. These energies were tapped to ensure the primacy of the Church of Rome and its growing political control as well.

This control by the Church culminated in the person of St. Bernard of Clairvaux. While not a Benedictine, he was an abbot of a Cistercian monastery at Clairvaux. He refused higher Church offices, but his obvious spirituality, his immense capacity of mind, will-power, and eloquence made him the most powerful man in Europe in the first half of the twelfth century. He was a maker and confidante of Popes, started the Second Crusade, and was a peacemaker among the rulers of western Europe. He consummated the art of combining the use spiritual power with political/physical power. This was a totally different use of spiritual energies than the builders of Stonehenge I had in mind.

My argument so far is that at least initially, ley lines were the result of building on power centers as a means of enhancing spiritual growth. At first there was no intent to build in straight lines; it just happened as a result of building on the underlying energy system. By 3000 BCE the awareness grew that we had been building sacred sites naturally in straight lines. Then came the first intentional alignments that did not coincide with energy leys. Initially, these too were made solely for spiritual purposes. The four-inch wide ley line at Avebury is an example of this. But the introduction of Iron Age hill forts and, later, Roman roads, Benedictine abbeys and Medieval castles as points on older ley lines indicates that Western Man was developing alternative uses for this phenomenon.

There isn't a specific date when the spiritual uses of ley lines ceased and the political/secular ones commenced, as there was a long period of over a thousand years when both were going on at the same time. And yet there are several examples of ecclesiastical leys in Medieval England. Brian Larkman, an Earth Mysteries researcher, has uncovered a ley line in York that, in addition to several other features, includes three churches, the magnificent York Minster, and the Deanery Chapter House all on that same ley! Five sacred structures on an energy ley; all have related primary water under them. In Oxford, Geomancer Nigel Pennick has found an ecclesiastical ley of seven churches, and apparently, the line goes through a different part of each of the seven churches.

But our days of conscious knowledge of the Earth Energies were numbered. Western Man insured that his linear objective consciousness would predominate by waging a systematic war of elimination against the intuitives and the Goddess. One of the first things that Constantine did after he made the Christian Church the state religion of the Roman

Empire was to genocidally root out the Gnostics, intuitives and followers of Christ who demanded the right to hear and interpret God's word for themselves. No one was to be allowed to think for themselves, to define their relationship with Christ for themselves.

Heresies and the Witch Trials

As the Dark Ages went on, the Church found more and more ways to deny the people access to spiritual realms. These attacks culminated in atrocities that are similar to America's genocidal war on the Native Americans, or Stalin's decimation of dissidents in Russia. If the treatment of those people the Church called heretics or witches had occurred anywhere else on Earth other than in supposedly civilized Europe, modern historians would have called the torture and burnings at the stake truly barbaric acts of primitive savages.

The last time that human sacrifice was practiced in Europe was during the witchcraft persecutions. Witches were perceived as a threat by the Church for several reasons. They were the remnant of the Goddess-centered religion who used power centers and incantations to connect with the spiritual *without going through the Church*. Also, its Earth Mother-centered path was at variance with the Church's patriarchal mode of operation.

The Medical Profession Lends a Hand

In the villages of the Middle Ages, it was women who provided the medical care. These healers knew about things like herbs and spells. Many were also midwives. This became a threat to a new professional class of men that was arising — doctors. "I've just been through five years of classes at the University to be a doctor. How can this untrained woman know anything about delivering babies?" The medical profession joined the Church in the persecution of witches (read: women, and mostly lower class). Western Man continued to burn witches/women at the stake up into the seventeenth century. In Salem, Massachusetts, they were killing women called witches in 1692. The last woman in Scotland to be killed for being a witch was put to death in 1722.

Eventually they had run out of lower class women, so they began to go for the upper class wives. But with the seventeenth century came the Age of Rationalism. An aristocratic husband could now argue, "What are you picking on my wife for? You know those realms don't rationally

exist anyway!" So the persecutions ceased, and the knowledge of the
Earth Energies faded away.

Dowsing as Heresy

It's easy to see how dowsing got into trouble. It is potentially a spiritual
tool that doesn't have to go through the Church to get answers. As
dowsing was thought to be a craft practised by witches, it fell into
extreme disfavor. It had been practised through the ages by those who
were in tune with the deeper harmonies of the Earth Energies, but
dowsing was a direct challenge to the patriarchal linear thinking and
rational methodology of Western Man and his Church — especially
when it was used as a tool for direct personal perception of the spiritual.
Dowsing had to be stamped out. Only its use as a tool to locate
drinking water was deemed to be so essential that dowsing for it had to
be allowed to remain as an acceptable channel to intuitive knowledge.

> Speaking of dowsing, have you done any since you began
> reading this chapter? Why not? I would trust that you would have
> your pendulum right by you as you read these pages. If you come
> to parts that don't seem quite right, check it with your pendulum.
> Remember, "This is what I want to do. Can I? May I? Am I ready?"
>
> By the way, where is the nearest power center to where you
> live? Where's the nearest point from your home where primary
> water and at least one energy ley come together?
>
> If you don't know, did you see a place in your mind's eye when
> you first read that last sentence? Did you feel some place? You
> probably already **know** where that place is. We'll be talking
> about dowsing at your power center a bit later, but let's get back
> to the alignments. Please remember to use your pendulum to
> verify for yourself the accuracy of what I am saying.

Pseudo-geomancy

While Western Man had forgotten about the Earth Energies that were
associated with the earlier ley lines, men all over Europe were still
creating intentional alignments to visually emphasize important buildings and monuments. As we shall see, this was not done to enhance the
spiritual potential of the sites at all, but rather to glorify the ego or to
enhance the power of specific individuals or groups who built them. It
was pseudo-geomancy (pseudo = false, geomancy = locating wo/
man-made structures in harmony with the Earth Spirit/Energies).

Gamla Upsala

Gamla (Old) Upsala is the Viking center in Sweden where all the early kings were crowned. There are mounds there dedicated to Woden, Thor and Freya (Wednesday, Thursday and Friday) that look for all the world like small Silbury Hills — conical in shape with flat tops. The Earth Energies are there, clearly indicating that the Vikings of the second half of the first millenium after Christ knew about them. Of primary importance is the water that is found as domes, or blind springs, under each mound. This is the Earth Mother. Dowseable energy leys cross over the primary water at the tops of the mounds.

In the distance one can easily see the spires of the Lutheran Cathedral at Upsala. This enormous brick building dominates the countryside. At one time this Cathedral town was also the capital of Sweden, but the center of political authority was later moved to Stockholm. However, the Upsala Cathedral is still the heart of the state religion in that country.

The spiritual authority was transferred to Upsala from Gamla Upsala in the middle of the second millenium after Christ. One piece of evidence of this transfer is that in Gamla Upsala, the bones of St. Eric were taken out each spring, and carried ceremonially around the fields to ensure a good harvest. This ritual to ensure fertility had been originally a Pagan rite of the Vikings. When the Vikings were first converted, the Christians, as they did everywhere they went, Christian-ized some of the Pagan practices. Christian St. Eric's bones replaced the Pagan fertility rites at Gamla Upsala. These bones have now been moved to the Upsala Cathedral. The power shifted.

There are two alignments that connect Gamla Upsala, the old center of power, with the Lutheran Cathedral, the new one. First some terms. The *major axis* of a Cathedral is determined by drawing a line from the center of the front door at the foot of the nave, to the center of the high altar (usually found at the opposite end of the building). The *minor axis* of any sacred site is a line that is perpendicular to the major axis.

A line drawn between the two magnificent spires that top Upsala's Cathedral would be a minor axis. They are aligned so that only one spire can be seen from the mounds at Gamla Upsala. The further spire is hidden behind the closer one. And yet, there is no energy ley that connects the two.

Second, just like a Roman road in Britain, there is a perfectly straight stretch of road at least three miles in length leading from the old center of power to the newer Cathedral. The road is just west of the mounds at

Gamla Upsala, and it aligns on those same two spires – but in this case, you can clearly see both of them. From this point on (the middle of the second millenium CE), we will see more and more use of straight roads used to draw the eye to the proclaimed center of physical power. There is no energy ley on this road either.

And yet, while there are these obvious visual alignments on the newer Cathedral, when one dowses the structure itself, there is no cohesive pattern of Earth Energies there, and no energy leys at all! And while there are occasional veins of underground water, they run randomly through the Cathedral, and none are to be found under the high altar. Primary water at sacred sites assumes very distinctive patterns. Veins enter and exit at significant points of the sacred enclosure. Those patterns are not there at the Cathedral. No energy ley crosses the high altar. The evidence is clear. The Vikings knew about the Earth Energies, the Swedish Lutherans didn't.

Versailles

Versailles, the Palace of Louis the XIV, is another example of pseudo-geomancy. Built in the seventeenth century at staggering expense to the French people, this monument to a monarch's enormous ego is made obvious by all of the roads leading in straight lines to the palace itself. This power trip of Louis' was a two-way affair. He not only received power from all of France in the form of homage given him by the various noblemen who fell over themselves to be seen at his court, but also Versailles was a visual center from which the power of the king emanated into the rest of the country. "The state is me," said Louis XIV. (Read: "I am the power, and make no mistake about that!")

So with Versailles we have a center of physical power, a magnificent edifice with many visual alignments converging on it. And yet, my pendulum tells me that while there are two energy leys within the confines of the palace and gardens, they are in no way related to the straight roads that lead to the palace, and neither energy ley crosses through the palace itself. Like the veins of water that are found in Upsala Cathedral, the energy leys there are random in terms of the construction.

What does your pendulum tell you about this?

The architects utilized the visual strength of alignments, but they were not backed by the real power. The Earth Energies are not there. The alignments at Versailles were constructed in part to focus the political power in France on the king, and as a center from which that controlling power then radiated back out into the country.

Pseudo-geomancy in Britain

In Britain, there are also examples of pseudo-geomancy. Paul Devereux, Editor of *The Ley Hunter*, and Director of the Dragon Project, told me of one in London in Kensington Gardens. There's a holy well there that has leading from it a straight path through the trees that runs to a church in Bayswater that was built in the 1850's, an obvious visual alignment. While there are clear yin energies associated with the holy well, there is no dowseable energy ley that runs on the path between the well and the church, and there are no cohesive Earth Energies at the church itself — no dome of water or blind spring under the altar, and no energy leys along the major axis of the church. /EXERCISE/
Check it yourself.

In Butleigh, a small village near Glastonbury, there is another example of pseudo-geomancy that begins near the village with two rows of impressive trees called Cedar Avenue. This stately avenue of Cedars of Lebanon begins near an old mansion in Butleigh, and draws the eye to the sky line where a massive cylindrical stone tower stands on the nearby Polden hills. While the avenue does draw the eye to the monument, it is not exactly aligned to it. As for the column itself, it was built by the Lord of the Manor, Samuel Hood, as a monument to his own gallantry while serving as an Admiral under Nelson. Like Versailles, there are no Earth Energies directly associated with it. In fact, when my daughter Jordan and I dowsed the base of the monument, we found only one vein of primary water running up to one outside corner of the iron fence that surrounds the base of the tower. The vein then turns in a loop and goes away from the monument, back in the direction it came from! The Earth Mother obviously wants nothing to do with this early nineteenth century pseudo-geomancy.

What we are seeing here is a time of forgetting. The reality of spiritual realms was being replaced by earthly desires to enhance individual power or ego. By the time of the Industrial Revolution, Western Man no longer seemed to remember the true significance of straight lines running across the surface of the Earth. He still built in straight lines, but these alignments were no longer ley lines. They had nothing to do with spiritual awareness or the Earth Energies.

But not everyone had forgotten.

Even As the Light Was Going Out,
It Was Coming On Again.

In the American Colonies in 1692, at the same time that they were
putting women to death for witchcraft in Salem, Massachussetts,
Johannes Kelpius, founder of one of the Rosicrucian orders in America
(AMORC), was building an underground meditation chamber in Fair-
mount Park, near Philadelphia in Pennsylvania. It is oriented due south
and sits on a power center.

Another example is the Wood family, residential architects of Bath in
England. Father and son, both with the name John Wood, changed the
face of that city in the eighteenth century. They built the Royal
Crescent, a massive sickle-shaped building complex that was designed to
house all classes of people who lived in Bath. The handle of the sickle
aligns with Kings Circus, a beautiful circular open space also in that city.
An energy ley runs concurrently with that alignment. Also, the Woods
demonstrated their awareness of true geomancy when they architect-
urally hooked their buildings in Bath into the Via Badonica, the Roman
road that goes to London. Along the way, the road/ley skirts the edge
of Silbury Hill, part of the Avebury complex.

Peru

Other cultures were still intimately involved with these energies. At the
beginning of the sixteenth century CE, when the Spaniards arrived in
Cusco, the capital of the Inca Empire in Peru, they found that there were
forty-one lines, or *ceques* that radiated out from the Coricancha, a major
temple in that city. The *ceques* not only carried on for miles into the
countryside, but dotted along these lines were holy places called *huacas*.
All of these huacas have primary water under them. Eleven of the
forty-one lines have energy leys running concurrently with them.

Check this yourself.

Ceques with their *huacas* are Peruvian ley lines.

Native Americans are also still in tune with these energies. The Hopi in
Arizona with their sacred Kivas know about it, and the Iroquois of New
York locate their Medicine Wheels and other sacred places at power
centers. One of my teachers is Twylah Nitsch, Clan Mother of the Wolf
Clan of the Seneca Nation of the Iroquois. The first time I arrived at her
teaching lodge I found her overseeing the construction of a Medicine
Wheel made out of slices of the trunk of an old maple tree. I dowsed an

energy ley slashing through the wheel, and a dome of water right in the center with the five veins swirling away in a widdershins, or anti-clockwise direction. Each of the veins exited the Medicine Wheel under one of the slices of maple. As with all truly sacred places, the points where veins of primary water exited the Medicine Wheel were clearly marked.

Perhaps the most interesting aspect of this is that at that time, Twylah didn't know how to dowse. She just "knew" where to place the wheel. She didn't need an external tool; she had the answer inside.

The Medicine Wheel

Feng Shui

In Hong Kong there are people today who still practice the ancient Chinese art of geomancy called Feng Shui. A geomancer's job is to locate buildings and sites all over the countryside in such a way that all is in harmony with the Earth Energies. Within the last several hundred years Feng Shui was practiced throughout China. At that time, nothing was allowed to interfere with the flow of the Earth Energies to the Emperor. Cemeteries had their place as did shrines, meeting places and homes.

In the travelling that I've done, I've never found primary veins or any other kind of Earth Energy that was detrimental to a person's health under any habitation site of any people whose culture was obviously working with these Energies. From the Neolithic village in Orkney called Skara Brae, through the many Bronze Age hut circles on Dartmoor in southwestern England, to American habitation sites of the Adena and Hopewell people (builders of the great geometrical earthworks and famous Serpent Mound in Ohio), and the homes of the Inca residents of Machu Picchu high in the Andes, these people never built their homes over these life detracting powers. Today, Western Man does it all the time, as in the "cancer houses" in Germany, with their deadly veins of underground primary water.

Neo-geomancy

But as the night seems darkest just before the dawn, the most malefic use of the alignments and the Earth Energies came in the first part of the twentieth century. As part of Adolph Hitler's Aryan Race Master Plan, various Nazi units began to research folk customs and geomancy; first to learn more about their Aryan forefathers, and later, to attempt to control Europe geomantically. In *"Germanien"*, a Nazi Germanic Culture magazine, there were articles by people like Josef Heinsch who wrote about things called *heilige linien* (holy lines) that were remarkably similar to Watkins' ley lines.

Nigel Pennick, a British Earth Mysteries luminary, in his book, *Hitler's Secret Sciences*, spoke of the *Deutsche Ahnenerbe* — the German Ancestral Heritage Organization. It was set up to study the spirit of the people, the lands which the "Nordic Indo-Germanic" (Aryan) race inhabited, and also to get other Germans interested and involved in this study. One member of the Ahnenerbe was Wilhelm Teudt, author of the Nazi Earth Mysteries bible, *Ancient German Sanctuaries*. Teudt actually headed the Ahnenerbe for a while, and he worked closely with Heinrich Himmler, head of the dreaded Nazi SS. Teudt visited Himmler at Wewelsburg, the SS's Grail Castle in Saxony.

The circular Nordturm (North Tower) of this geomantically designed triangular castle was said to be "the center of the earth." Built mostly by slave labor, Wewelsburg was set up to support the Nazi Aryan race doctrines. It was set geomantically into the landscape with the rest of the town radiating out from the focal point of the Nordturm. It was like Versailles, only much more sinister. And the Earth Energies were there as well.

Himmler, Albert Speer, Hitler's architect, and other Nazis experimented with geomancy throughout Europe in an attempt to control that part of the world and the entire continent. The *Führerhauptquartier Wolfsschanze*, Hitler's main headquarters and the site of the unsuccessful bomb plot against him, was intentionally constructed on an ancient holy well, at the crossing of two ley lines.

One classic example of the Nazi's use of geomancy happened during the German rush to take Moscow. At one point, a detachment of Mountain Troops was diverted to place the Nazi flag on top of a strategically unimportant mountain, Mount Elbruz. The Persians, good Aryan stock, believed that Mount Elbruz was a world mountain, center of the Earth Energies. Himmler felt that if the Nazi swastika controlled Elbruz, they could better control the Russians. As far as the Third Reich's march on Moscow was concerned, it made no sense at all to divert troops way down into the Caucusus, but geomantically, for the Nazis, it was of major importance.

The Allied Psycho/Spiritual Counterattack

The Third Reich repeatedly used alignments for psychic control and to enhance their physical power. They intended to dominate the world. When it was realized how heavily the Nazis were into astrology, the Allies began to use astrologers as well in an attempt to figure out what Hitler was up to. Thankfully there were also adepts on the Allied side who worked to undo the damage of this insane megalomaniac and his black magicians. Wellesley Tudor Pole, who later did such good work at the Chalice Well Gardens in Glastonbury, initiated the Silent Minute in Britain in World War II. Each evening at nine, as Big Ben chimed the hour, all of Britain stopped for one minute and focused their energies to pray for peace. This moment, when all of Britain was as one, created an especially clear channel between the visible and invisible worlds. The spiritual realms were more than willing to come to the aid of those who fought against men who would use the Earth Energies to conquer the world. What a powerful tool for psychically uniting a people! Most people don't seem to realize how much of World War II was fought on these spiritual levels. What we have seen throughout the history of alignments is a steady decline from the spiritual to the physical in the use of these linear features culminating in the malevolent applications and sinister uses of the Earth Energies by the Nazis in World War II.

Dod at Stonehenge

Western Man vs. Indigenous Peoples

Western Man continues to treat power centers and sacred places with ignorance that adds to their destruction. In the Four Corners of the American Southwest, the Hopi Indians live a life that has been essentially the same for five hundred years. One of the major power centers of the United States is said to be there along with the Hopi Kivas (underground temples) and the breathing mountains — sacred mountains that inhale air at certain times of day and exhale it at other times. This way of life and the sanctity of the land is threatened by uranium miners.

In Australia near a town called Jabiru, the aborigines have an especially important sacred site called Djibi Djibi. There are at least three hundred rock paintings, and a myth/story about what would happen if someone took the serpent out of that area. Like the Four Corners of the U.S., Jabiru is at the heart of uranium country. No respect. I want my electricity at all costs.

Dowsing and Archeology

In addition to uranium miners, sacred places are also being desecrated by archeologists. In the past few years I have changed my mind about using dowsing to help archeologists locate artifacts at cemeteries and *sacred* sites. In the mid-seventies, I worked on a dig for the National Geographic Society in the New England State of Vermont where we excavated four underground chambers, quite similar to the fougous and souterrains of the British Isles. Peter Reynolds, the leader of the excavation, had done some dowsing himself, so he was open to my using this art to help him to decide where to dig. I must say now, with the vantage of hindsight, I would no longer use my dowsing skills to do this.

Native Americans and the Anthros

Floyd Westerman is a Native American Indian who belongs to the Sisseton-Wahpeton Dakota (Sioux) Nation. He sings songs about his people and their history. In his tape, "Custer Died For Your Sins", he has a cut entitled, "Here Come the Anthros". The first line sets the tone, "And the Anthros (Anthropologists) keep on commin' like death and taxes to our land." Towards the end of the song he makes the point that really speaks to me:

> "*And the Anthros keep on diggin'*
> *in our sacred ceremonial sites.*
> *As if there was nothing wrong,*
> *and their education*
> *gives them the right.*"

I wonder what the reaction would be if a crack team of highly trained anthropologists and archeologists were to come from Japan to do a superbly planned dig at Arlington National Cemetery in Washington, or at Westminster Abbey in London? How long would that be tolerated? And yet it is perfectly all right for any university in the United States to dig in any Native American graveyard they want to. What's the difference? "... As if there was nothing wrong, and their education gives them the right." Human beings are human beings, and grave robbing is grave robbing whether the goods end up in a museum or someone's home. There's a Sioux woman who told an Iroquois friend of mine that the anthros had already dug up her grandmother.

Let's look at another example. Willhelm Reich was a student of Freud's who became interested in the energy of the orgasm. He came to believe that this energy was a powerful manifestation of our life force, and he called it *orgone*. Dowsing indicates a similarity between ley energy and orgone. Reich found that layers of organic and inorganic materials (he used wool blankets and steel wool) concentrated this orgone. Unfortunately, he ran afoul of the Food and Drug Administration when he built large boxes called *orgone accumulators* and told people that it might cure their cancer if they sat in one. But that's another story.

Archeological Rape

The Boyne Valley in northeastern Ireland has a spectacular collection of passage graves – Newgrange, Dowth, and Knowth – not to mention the earliest ley lines that I have seen. At the moment, from my humble point of view, archeologists are in the process of raping Knowth. There are enormous gashes at several points in the flanks of that ancient and holy mound. Black plastic is everywhere. Even from the observation platform behind the barbed wire walls (it felt like Berlin where I spent three years), one could clearly see that the mound was constructed of layers – layers of sod and rock – layers of organic and inorganic material.

Have you ever participated in a dig? If you have, you will know that when they are digging, archeologists are very very careful. As they work their way down, they look at every layer almost centimeter by centimeter. But what happens when the dig is over? Do they put it back the way they found it? No. They do what is called backfilling. All you need is muscles and a big shovel – or in this case, probably a bulldozer.

It is claimed that they're saving Knowth. Oh it might look more pretty when they're through, but from a functional point of view, they're destroying it. Just as nearby "restored" Newgrange where the tunnel was encased in positive ion generating cement, this dig at Knowth is being done for science and the tourists – not for the pilgrims.

Stenness is a henge monument (ditch and bank) in the Orkney Islands north of Scotland. While there are several smaller stones, there are only three of the truly massive stones in that circle left. They're over twenty feet high, seven feet wide, and only nine inches thick.

As Stenness is over five thousand years old, it is not surprising that the ditch and bank are so eroded as not to really be visible any more. Some archeologist/bureaucrat with his eye firmly focused on the tourist dollar somehow got the money to bring in fill to make a phoney bank!

When I was up there in the autumn of 1985, they were bringing in the fill by the truck load. Even the Orcadians who had been hired to do the work thought that it was "a shame."

Please do not infer that I am opposed to all archeology and all dowsing for artifacts. This is not the case. There are more and more archeologists who are becoming sensitive to these issues. In New England, Byron Dix and James Mavor reported in the December 1983 "Bulletin of the Early Sites Research Society" about a dig they did at a site in Freetown, Massachusetts. Dotted with over one-hundred stone mounds and several stone rows, this important Native American ceremonial center was about to become the site of the new hazardous waste treatment plant for the New Bedford watershed. In order to bring the ritual nature of this site to public attention, and to try to stop the proposed desecration of the land, Byron and Jim first surveyed the site, and decided to dig just one of the mounds to see if they could find evidence that could stop the site from being usurped by the hazardous waste treatment plant. As they say in their paper, "Chief Little Horse of the Wollomonopaug Indian Tribal Council performed a traditional ritual of respect prior to our excavation of the selected stone mound." The significant amounts of red ochre, crude stone tools, and radio carbon dates of 875 ± 160 and 790 ± 150 years before 1950 CE (the year all carbon dates are correlated to) added a great deal of weight to the argument that these stone cairns were definitely not the result of erratic colonial field clearing! This kind of sensitivity and respect are what we need much more of in the field of archeology. To dig a sacred site one needs permission from more than just the present landowner or from some state bureaucrat.

There are times when it is totally appropriate for dowsers to assist archeologists in locating artifacts in a dig of an early Industrial Revolution site, and probably even at the habitation sites (homes) like those of the Native American encampments found along many of the rivers, or at the hut circles of Iron Age Britain. It's the sacred sites that I'm worried about protecting. The cemeteries. The temples. In the Bible it's called holy ground. Incidentally I would dowse holy ground for artifacts if say a Motorway or Interstate Highway were coming through. Rescue archeology is a laudable effort and should be supported. But normally, there are many less intrusive ways of recovering information about these sacred spaces than by digging.

With the few exceptions mentioned above, I will no longer use my dowsing skills to help archeologists dig at any places of spiritual import. I urge other Earth Mystery dowsers on the spiritual path to consider quite carefully the implications of using dowsing for any archeological excavation of sacred space.

The Limitations of the Scientific Model

The history of the use and misuse of alignments is clear: the closer to the present we get, the more Western Man abused the power of alignments for his own personal gain. Therefore, to look at sacred space from only Western Man consciousness (read: using only the scientific model) will only lead to further error and further descent into the physical. For example, we must not fall prey to science's demand for the repeatability of an experiment. Modern physics in general has taught us that the observer is just as much a part of the experiment as anything else. The presence of a totally objective, uninvolved/unevolved, skeptical observer actually mitigates against repeatablilty when working in these realms.

Scientists also love the fact that dowsing isn't always accurate or repeatable because then they get to discredit the whole process: to throw the baby out with the bath water. Because different dowsers don't come up with the same things at any given site, they decide dowsing is an invalid tool. Maybe, maybe not. We're just relearning how to use these tools. Because we are not perfectly realized beings, dowsing isn't right one hundred percent of the time. But it could also be that, like the proverbial three blind men, each of us is "seeing" a slightly different part of the elephant. According to our individual level of consciousness, as each of us takes our first faltering steps into a realm where Baconian physics doesn't seem to work, we each return to tell slightly different stories of our experiences. We will find different things. And that's ok.

God is Good
– Old Saying

If good is the opposite of evil,
then it's not Good.
– Krishnamurti

Dowsing and the Devil

There is another group of people who are non-dowsers who have something to say about the fact that dowsing isn't always correct. Fundamentalist Christians posit that the forces of darkness, demons, move the rod. It can't possibly be God who moves the stick because God is perfect, and He wouldn't lie. So since a dowser's findings aren't always correct, an imperfect force (the Devil) is moving it. I must admit that logically, this is a powerful argument, but as we all look through a glass darkly, there are other ways to "see" this elephant, other paradigms. Fundamentalists put the cause of the inaccuracies outside with demons; I would suggest that it's an internal problem.

One way of looking at what it means to be human is that by definition, we are imperfect. As an imperfect being, I am intent on growing spiritually — towards perfection. And while I intend to grow closer to the One, I also recognize that there are forces that pull in the opposite direction. The Hindus call this force Maya or Illusion. It *is* possible through dowsing to contact this force of Illusion, and obviously, spiritual dowsers need to be aware of this. Knowing this, I intend that my dowsing answers come only from our Creator, from Love. But there's a problem here. Our bodies are the temples for our Soul and for the Spirit that is in us, but unfortunately, like Hercules at the Augean Stables (and you know what they were full of), our temples need some serious house-cleaning. If one sees dowsing as receiving answers from the Omniscient Perfect Source, then it is our own personal lack of cleanliness that makes the static, that causes incorrect dowsing responses. To make our bodies proper temples for our Souls and the Spirit that comes in with every breath (re*spir*ation), we've got to clean up our own acts. (This is called throwing stones when I live in a glass house myself.) It is our own imperfection that makes it impossible for Perfection to come through perfectly.

It's like any new terrain. From the earliest humans as they moved out of their caves, (or the Garden depending on your point of view), to the astronaut walking on the Moon for the first time, pioneers know that there are risks. It's true with any new venture. But by focusing on the One, or Christ, or the Goddess, or Krishna, or YHVH, or the Great Spirit, or whatever you call the best you can imagine, you can consciously grow in your awareness of the spiritual realms.

John White, a Christian writer in the "Spiritual Frontiers Fellowship Journal" (Vol XII, Autumn 1980) writes:

"*The importance of Jesus was not that he was a human like us but that we are gods like him — or at least we have the evolutionary potential to be.*

"... the cosmic calling we humans have will not be denied forever, despite the ignorance of religious institutions. The Holy Spirit will simply move on to new forms, leaving fossils behind."

Overview of Alignments

Let's take a step back for an overview of the whole herstory/history of alignments. The earliest ley lines were not intentional alignments of sites; they were accidental/coincidental alignments of sites. They just happened as a result of our building sacred sites on power centers. They ran concurrently with the energy leys.

These early alignments all had close spiritual connections. Slowly, with the inclusion of the defensive Iron Age hill forts and later Roman roads, the use of alignments to enhance physical power began to intrude on the earlier holy alignments. In the British Isles, there was a several-thousand-year period of interface between the spiritual and physical use of alignments — from roughly 800 BCE to 1300 CE.

There was a much more recent time when men (and it was men, not women) created intentional alignments to indicate where the governmental power was, or to aggrandize a specific individual's ego. These pseudo-geomancers had forgotten about the Earth Energies — the real reason for those alignments in the first place. With the Neo-geomancers of Hitler's Third Reich we see the use of alignments taken to their logical, linear, left-brained extreme.

The implication here is that, from an ethical point of view, as we are once again trying to learn about these mysteries, it is inappropriate to use only the scientific method. The over-emphasis on only the linear rational approach in the use of alignments just to enhance physical power culminates in Hitler's interest in geomancy. To continue employing *only* the scientific method to learn about sacred space is therefore not only a very limiting but ethically suspect approach. If spiritual growth (rather than physical power) is the goal, there needs to be much more of a wholistic way to become involved in these mysteries.

No wonder most archeologists and anthropologists today are unable to conceive of the possibility that the knowledge of ley lines existed at all, let alone there being an ongoing continuity of the system in Europe from before 3000 B.C. to about the time of the Protestant Reformation! To a rational academic mind, such a thread of continuity seems impossible and inconceivable. This was one of Bellamy and Williamson's major blindspots in their book, *Ley Lines In Question*. They insisted that ley lines consist only of Neolithic sites. This example of totally linear thinking, and its concomitant lack of awareness of the reality of the spiritual, leads to academia's inability to comprehend the possibility of spiritually aware Europeans knowing of these linear energy leys for over four thousand years. Conveniently forgetting that the Church and other representatives of Western Man waged a thousand year war against those who knew about these energies, academia can smugly say, "I mean after all, let's be rational about this. If ley lines were that important, why aren't they in the written record?"

New Skills for the Ley Hunter

We have also seen various examples of alignments that were created specifically to enhance domination over others on the physical plane. Power over. Not all alignments of sites can be called ley lines. To tell the difference, in addition to their use of compass, sighting, and mapping skills, ley hunters must also become competent water dowsers, as primary water is found under every valid marker of the ley system. Alfred Watkins' ley lines mark the Earth Energies. If those Energies aren't there, they may be intentional alignments, but they're not ley lines. They are examples of pseudo-geomancy. During a period when geomantic awareness was fading, they are but a vestigial remnant of a time when humanity knew of this power in our Earth. Even so, these recent alignments are yet another piece of evidence that is beginning to show quite convincingly to those who have eyes to see, that throughout herstory, cultures here in Europe (and in other parts of the world) were well aware of the power of the straight line.

The Light Turns Back On

The First Ley Hunter – William Pidgeon

In 1853, William Pidgeon was the first English speaking person in modern times (read: Western Man) to notice and to record that ancient peoples constructed their sacred sites in straight lines. Pidgeon was taken through the Ohio and Mississippi river valleys of the United States by an old Indian, De-Coo-Dah, the last Medicine Man of the Elk Nation. Pidgeon was shown all kinds of massive earthworks including geometrical shapes and animal or human shapes that were referred to as effigies, or effigy mounds. He wrote about his exploits in his book *De-Coo-Dah*. In talking about the reasons why he believed that these earthworks were all built by the same people, Pidgeon cited similar construction techniques and said:

"This conclusion is further established by the extensive ranges of mounds, extending sometimes in *direct and continuous lines for several hundred miles* (emphasis mine), consisting of truncated mounds, occasionally varied by effigies, or works of singular form and arrangement.

"... And there is little doubt that these ranges were constructed as division lines, or land-marks between adjacent territories, kingdoms, or tribes. This is evident, not only from the vast extent of territory which these lines include, but from the character of the symbols or effigies which are always found at points where the principle lines intersect each other, or are joined by lines diverging laterally as seen in Iowa, Wisconsin and Circleville, Ohio.

"After having, in company with De-Coo-Dah, traced several extensive lines of mounds through Wisconsin and Iowa, in the fall of 1849, I visited Circleville in Ohio, with the design of testing the truth of tradition respecting the union of lineal ranges (Pidgeon's term for ley lines) at that point.... But the junction of the Great Miami River having been traditionally named as the western terminus of one of the diverging ranges, we assumed a geographical line between that point and Circleville, and soon succeeded in discovering a well-defined mound about two miles north of Paint Creek, in Fayette County.... We proceeded west, to the headwaters of the east fork of Todd's Fork of the Little Miami, where we discovered the third work of the range, in a cultivated field about one half of a mile southeast of Wilmington, Clinton County; thence we proceeded west to the junction of Todd's Fork with the Miami, about one and a half miles north of which, on the west side of that river, we found the fourth work. We then, with the assistance of a pocket-compass, retraced the line, and became fully convinced that it was, in fact, a lineal range."

It is clear that these "lineal ranges" marked off territories (in England, many ley lines mark parish boundaries). Points that marked these alignments in Ohio had ceremonial rather than defensive military purposes. There is primary water under each of the markers. They are ley lines.

> Check your pendulum to see if there were energy leys on
> Pidgeon's range lines as well.

Norman Lockyer

At the beginning of this century Astronomer Norman Lockyer was studying ancient sites in terms of their relationship with the Sun, Moon and stars. He worked in Egypt as well as in Britain, and is considered to be the founder of what Americans call archeoastronomy, and the British call astroarchaeology. At Stonehenge, he not only studied the Summer Solstice Sunrise that occurs along the major axis, but he also noticed the alignment with Old Sarum, Salisbury Cathedral and Clearbury Camp that we discussed earlier. He found other alignments down in Land's End in Cornwall, an area that John Michell was to study so intensively sixty years later.

Alfred Watkins

The term "ley" meaning this alignment of sacred sites was coined in the nineteen-twenties by Alfred Watkins in his book, *The Old Straight Track*. Watkins was an incredibly talented Englishman who, among other things, invented a photo-electric meter that for the first time allowed a photographer to know exactly how to set her/his aperture on the camera. He was also a salesman for his father's granary business, and developed a recipe for a particularly nutritious loaf of bread. He had the kind of mind that inquired into many different things. This is essential to a student of the Earth Mysteries.

In his travels for his father's business, Watkins had an on-going love affair with the Herefordshire countryside. He knew most of the people in the outlying regions, and enjoyed talking with them. His photographs of Herefordshire in the early part of this century are an important part of that region's historical record.

But it was for a daydream he had that we remember him most. On a Sunny day, while taking his rest at a scenic spot, Watkins had a revelation. The ancient sites which he saw lined up in straight lines! All over the countryside, like a giant web, these straight lines connected the old holy sites — standing stones, dolmens (perched rocks), notches in hills, church spires, stone rows, logan stones (rocking rocks), round and long barrows, hill forts, and stone rings. A group called the Old Straight Track Club was formed to investigate these alignments, and continued his work for the next several decades.

The work of Alfred Watkins in the rediscovery of the ley system is seminal; however, as with Sigmund Freud, the founder of modern psychiatry, it is possible to build, refine and expand upon the work of both men. Not all of the ley lines that Alfred Watkins described in *The Old Straight Track* have energy leys running along them, but there is primary water – either a dome/blind spring, or a crossing of veins that exit out of the corners – under every valid marker on a ley. These alignments were used for spiritual purposes.

The Early Earth Energy Dowsers

Reginald Allender Smith was Keeper of both the British and Egyptian Antiquities at the British Museum. He also was a secret dowser. When he retired in the nineteen-thirties, he came out of the closet, so to speak, and gave a lecture which appeared in the *Journal of the British Society of Dowsers* in which he claimed to find water under all of the ancient sacred places.

Guy Underwood, in an enigmatic little book, *The Pattern of the Past*, wrote about various yin, Earth Mother Energies other than underground water, though perhaps his "water lines" had some connection with veins of underground primary water that we have been looking at. It is interesting to note that as a dowser, he could not find energy running along the leys. It is a good example of the oft repeated experience of the dowsers going to the same sites and finding different things. While this is a very important book on the Earth Energies, it is hard to get, and rather difficult to understand. I would recommend that you read it about tenth on your list of Earth Mystery books.

The yang Earth Energies related to the ley system were also redis-covered in the nineteen-thirties. Author Dion Fortune, a Glastonbury mystic, was the first to suggest that there was some kind of energy running between sacred sites. These were the energy leys. Other dowsers soon picked up these energy leys as well. The two polarities of the Earth Energy system were now back in our consciousness.

In the nineteen-fifties Tony Wedd opened up the Earth Mysteries can of worms with his discovery that certain UFO sightings appeared to be in straight lines. He called them "orthotenies" (alignments of landed or low-level UFO sightings), and felt that there was also a connection with physical alignments of ancient sacred sites — Watkins' ley lines. John Michell's first book, *Flying Saucer Vision* in 1967 was about this connection.

Recent Earth Energy Work

Michell continued in the Seventies with a series of brilliant books, starting with *View Over Atlantis* and *City of Revelation*, that have influenced all students of the Earth Mysteries. He not only clarified Watkins' ley notion, but his book *The Old Stones of Land's End* on his work in Cornwall set new standards for accuracy and uniformity of culture. We've talked before about the anthropological fixation that ley lines must be of only one culture. It has been a blind spot of theirs for years. All of the points on Michell's Land's End ley lines in Cornwall are of Neolithic origin, but this is an exception to the rule. On most ley lines one finds examples of multiple cultural use.

Since the publication of *The Ley Hunter's Companion* with Ian Thompson in 1979, Paul Devereux has probably been the most influential person in the study of alignments. As Editor of *The Ley Hunter* magazine, Devereux has championed the necessity of accuracy in describing these ancient sacred alignments. Devereux's definition of ley lines is the standard to which those interested in terrestrial alignments of sacred sites in Britain must aspire. In *The Ley Hunter* No. 97 he writes, "Leys are straight at least to the standard of an "H" or harder pencil line on the 1:25,000 scale, and which are marked by definite prehistorical sites and confirmed pre-Reformation ecclesiastical structures (churches, abbeys, crosses, etc.). Moats, mottes, assigned sections of road, markstones, etc. should only be counted as secondary features on lines already marked by primary features. Keep leys as short as possible, under 10 miles if you can. Also ensure that you have visited all or most of the sites on a line, if not the course of the alignment between them. Carry out at least preliminary archive work, if only checking Pevsner's *Buildings in England*."

American ley hunters can't incorporate all of Devereux's suggestions (i.e. an American Pevsner wouldn't go back far enough, and U.S. Geodetic Survey Maps are of too big a scale), but his methodology for determining ley lines applies anywhere in the world. Ultimately a ley line has to be a very straight and narrow line that is marked along its length by pre-Western-Man-constructed spiritual centers or holy places.

Devereux's work as Director of the Dragon Project, centered at the Rollright Stone Circle in Oxfordshire, has opened up many new understandings, mostly in the scientific field, about the energies peculiar to sacred sites. His non-intrusive methodology of exploring these ancient sites has set a new standard for research into our prehistory.

The ASD Earth Mysteries Group

I first heard about ley lines and underground water in the late Sixties from Terry Ross when he spoke at length about the ley system that same weekend when I saw those figures in the white robes at the Calendar II chamber. He had worked with British dowsers at sacred sites, and brought his findings to the United States in the late Sixties and early Seventies. He is a master dowser, and in the mid-Seventies, he was one of my Field Faculty when I did my Masters work (post graduate) in Sacred Space.

As a result of my work with the ASD Earth Mysteries Group in Vermont, where we studied over thirty underground chambers like Calendar II, we discovered that the primary water that is found at any truly sacred space has a pattern to it that links it directly to the structure itself. For example, standing stones usually have two veins of primary water crossing underneath. The veins both enter and exit the stone at its corners.

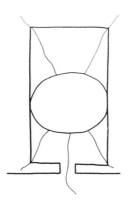

Calendar II Chamber Dome and Veins

Often there is also a connection between the diameter of the dome of water at a power center, and the width of the sacred structure that is placed on it. The diameter of the dome is equal to the width of the enclosure and fits exactly within it. I've seen this interrelationship between the primary water and the sacred architecture at an interior enclosed portion of Castle Rigg (a magnificent stone ring in the Lake District of England), at a Norman Chapel at Tintagel (said to be the birth place of King Arthur), in Glastonbury Abbey at the Mary Chapel (site of the first above-ground Christian church in the world), in passage graves in Ireland, at the Intihuatana Stone in Machu Picchu, and in many underground stone chambers in New England.

Sacred Space – Your First Visit

We come now to the point of thinking about how a dowser can best approach a sacred site or natural power center. But first, you need a power center to approach. If you already know of a stone ring, perched rock, circular grove of trees, standing stone, kiva, holy well or any other site of ancient sacredness near you, you're in business. You might even know of a natural power center – a place where the energy leys and primary water meet, but no one has apparently ever built on it.

> A while back I asked you where your nearest power center was. Has anything come to you about that issue since then? You might have seen it flash in your mind's eye. Perhaps an answer came in with a smell or a sound that reminded you of a certain nearby place. Use all of your physical senses to aid you in tuning in to the spiritual.
>
> If you haven't had a "hit" of where it is, and if level three dowsing works for you, try map dowsing. Get a map of the area, and lay it out on a table, put north away from you. Even if level three dowsing hasn't worked for you in the past, get your pendulum out – "I want to find out where my nearest power center is." "Can I?" "May I?" "Am I ready?" Please try this now.
>
> Assuming you have a "yes" so far, the next question you then need to ask is, "Is it on this map?" If the answer is "no", you need to get a larger scale map – one with less inches to the mile – so you can dowse a larger area. In any event, once you have the right map, and it is oriented with north being away from you, there are several ways you can proceed. (Remember, there's no right way of doing anything in dowsing. Do what works best for you.) I hold my pendulum over the point on the map where I am and ask it to point in the direction of the nearest power center. My search

position is back and forth. I watch the leading edge, the point of the pendulum's swing that is away from me. When I ask for direction, as the pendulum oscillates back and forth, the leading edge starts moving towards the left or right, and eventually stops and swings back and forth along a new line. The target is in that direction. As a check ask, "Is this direction correct? Is this the truth?"

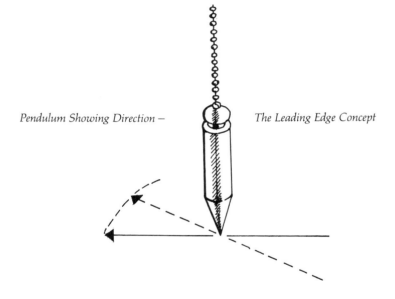

Pendulum Showing Direction –   *The Leading Edge Concept*

I then go along that line with my pendulum in the search position. As I approach the target, my pendulum will start to go into an ellipse. When I'm directly over the target, the pendulum will be going in a perfectly circular direction. I use map dowsing as an approximation to tell me when I am in the right area. I need to go out to the site to determine the exact location.

L Rods and Map Dowsing

L rods also work well. I like the ones with sleeves, and I hold them upside down, with the longer part of the L below my hands and just above the surface of the map. Starting with a clear statement of what my target is – the power center nearest to where I am now – I begin at the lower right-hand corner of the map and move the L rods up the right-hand edge – from south to north. When my hands come to the east-west line (exact latitude) which runs through the target, the rods will go out. When my fists are directly over that point, the rods will be perpendicular to the right-hand edge of the map. The L rod in my left hand is pointing due west, directly at the power center. I draw a line across the map at this point. Now I start at the upper right-hand edge of the map and go across the top – from east to west. Again, the left-hand rod points to the power center when both rods are in their full outstretched position. I draw another line on the map perpendicular to the edge at that point. The power center nearest to where I am is the point where these two lines intersect. See if you can figure out a way to map dowse the energies that are there. Is there primary water there? How many energy leys?

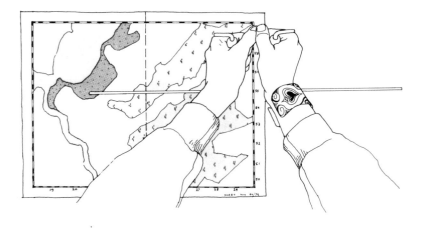

L Rods Held Upside Down for Map Dowsing

Once you have determined where the site is, go there. The pattern of your on-site dowsing will depend on why you are into the Earth Mysteries in the first place. Are you reading this book because you want to be able to convince someone else of the reality of these energies? Perhaps the scientific model of critical objectivity might be your first approach, but, as we have discussed above, this contains an element of danger. History teaches us that the odds are that you will ultimately be tempted to try to use this knowledge for inappropriate (read: unethical) gain on the physical level. For example, there are those who dream of using these spiritual life force energies to light a light bulb. Imagine the money you could make from that! A cheap source of energy....

See where that one leads? If you do see, but you're thinking, "Yeah, but think about our need for electricity ...," please think some more about it. The Earth Energies are here to support life itself and to help us to connect with the spiritual realms from which they come. To use it to make electricity would be like a Christian using pieces of Christ's cross as kindling to light a fire to keep warm. It would work, but it sure is an inefficient and inappropriate use of the Spirit.

But if you are using dowsing as a tool for spiritual growth and raising consciousness, and if you want to experience these energies for yourself, an attitude of respect and reverence would be more appropriate. This doesn't necessarily require solemnity; many spiritual experiences are full of laughter. You might also want to bring something as an offering — a pebble from some other site, or a flower. The Native Americans often bring tobacco for this purpose. The proper mental attitude, and a gift for the *genius loci* (the spirit of the place) enhance the possibility that you will contact the spiritual. They're like the witness chamber in some pendulums — it helps you focus on what you're looking for.

A friend of mine, Joe Jochmans, takes people to sacred sites in Egypt, Israel, Mexico, and Peru and other places. He usually takes a few moments before entering a site to hold hands in a circle with whomever he's with, and to say the following:

   1. We are filled with and protected by the divine light, love and spirit.
   2. We freely give a portion of that light as a gift to this place.
   3. We come with a desire to learn. Please fill up our cup, but not with more than is appropriate to our present level of development.

The first statement is a prayer of protection, "Great Spirit be with us." The second is much like the notion of bringing a flower or tobacco. You are bringing an offering to one of the gates of the spiritual realms. This also helps energize the site/gate as well. The third is a statement of intent. It says why you are there and that you don't want to blow your fuses. In the Hindu system, these fuses are called the *nadis*. I'm also reminded of the Lord's admonition to Moses on Mount Sinai not to look at Him because he wouldn't be able to handle it. Protection, an offering, and a statement of intent – a good way of preparing yourself to grow on spiritual levels.

Dowsing at a Power Center

As a dowser, you are now ready to look at the energies there. If there is a power center where you had thought, there will be primary water there as part of it. It is important to remember that it is not the water herself that is the yin energy we're interested in. Somehow, the cracks in our Mother's mantle (through which primary water flows) allow certain yin energies to come to the surface that are otherwise blocked by that mantle. When there is a crossing of veins or a dome, those yin energies can come to the surface even more easily. Holy wells give even better access to these Earth Mother energies. But don't confuse the water with the yin Earth Energy. Water on the surface or in streams or lakes is neutral, although waterfalls are excellent negative ion generators.

Primary Water

Holding a single L rod out in front of you in the search position, ask where the nearest power center is. Turn around slowly, and when it is pointing in the right direction, the tip of the rod will seem to stick. If you continue to turn, the tip will still point in that direction. Now with both rods out in the search position, ask them to cross at the center. Walk in that direction until they cross. If you've done everything right, you are over the power center.

At the power center, look for the water first. If it's a small power center like a single standing stone, there could be a crossing of veins with each vein entering or exiting out of a corner of the stone. If it's a bigger center, there will be a dome of water with an odd number of veins coming out of it. Locate the dome, and trace its circumference. A single L rod can do this quite well. Approach the edge of the dome asking the rod to tell you when you've reached it. When you get to the edge of it, the tip of the L rod will seem to stick to that edge. You can then walk around the circumference of the dome letting the tip of your rod lead you as a dog on a leash might lead her/his owner in looking for a rabbit.

S/he follows the dog. You follow the tip. As you walk, it will stick
to the edge. If you are on a wo/man-made site, does the
circumference of the dome fit in somehow to the layout of the
place?

Now pick up each vein and trace where it goes until it exits the
site. Few domes have more than five veins. The biggest dome I've
ever found was under Silbury Hill in Avebury. It has eleven veins.
Even so, if you find over five, you're probably finding too many.

Hermes/Mercury, the messenger of the gods and Trickster, has
long been associated with these quicksilver Earth Energies. He is
the hermit who helps travellers and pilgrims along the way. He
can trick you, or bring you messages from Olympus. Unfortunately
most dowsers encounter him first as the Trickster.

When the Trickster is up to his pranks, what you **think** you will
find, you **will** find every time unless you're careful. Are you really
clear that you have not had any expectations? Or were you
asking, "I wonder what it's going to be? I wonder what it's going
to be?" When you are convinced that you have done it correctly,
develop a picture of the pattern of the dome and her veins.

Dowsing the Energy Leys

Now for the energy leys, those six to eight foot wide perfectly
straight beams of yang energy that have a direction of flow.
Holding your L rods out in the search position, ask to find the
edges of any energy leys that are there. When you come to one,
your rods will start to go out. When the arms are exactly opposite
each other, stop. (A nice thing about using L rods for this work is
that no matter from what angle you approach the edge of a dead
straight energy ley, when the two arms are extended in line with
each other, your hands are not only at the edge of the ley, but
also the arms of the L rods show in what direction the energy ley
runs.) Notice that one L rod is pointing towards the dome, and
one the other away. Six to eight feet in front of you, you should
encounter the other edge. Continue on around the dome,
counting the energy leys as you go, until you get back to the first
energy ley you dowsed. Divide by two and that will give you the
number of energy leys at that crossing. (Remember that most leys
go directly through the power center, so you dowsed them twice
as you went around the circle.) If you come up with a number
and a half, say $3\frac{1}{2}$, it means that there are three energy leys that
cross through the power center, and another energy ley that,

depending on its direction of flow, either begins or ends there.

If you find two or more energy leys at a standing stone where you have previously dowsed a crossing of veins, something is probably wrong. I find a dome, or blind spring, at every power center with two or more energy leys. If you are on an ancient sacred site rather than on a natural power center, one of the energy leys that you dowsed will exit out of the major axis of the site. You can determine the direction of flow by standing in the center of the energy ley, and with a single L rod in the search position, ask, "Which way is downstream?" Turn in a circle as you did when you were initially finding the direction of the site, and the tip of the rod will stick in the direction that is downstream.

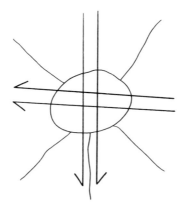

Dome and Two Energy Leys at a Power Center

The biggest problem that most beginning Earth Energy dowsers make is to confuse energy leys with what is actually underground water. The difference is very subtle at first, so if you pick up over two or three energy leys, get suspicious. If you find over five and a half you are either on one of the most important sacred points on the face of this Earth, or you are wrong. Suspect the Trickster. I've never been honored to visit a site with over five and a half. There does appear to be a connection with the notion of the more energy leys, the more powerful a site is, but I have had marvellous times on a single ley.

Other Ways To Perceive the Energy

As far as spiritual development is concerned, the number of leys, or where they are isn't that important. The issue is that they are there, and that you know where they cross over the dome. That is where you want to put your body, or if you are with friends, to make your circle. This is Union.

Don't go only with the movement of the dowsing tool. The ultimate goal is to get rid of them anyway. How does the site feel? Is there a particular emotion that comes up for you? Does your body tell you anything? Can you feel it in your knees or feet? Others experience it in their stomach or some other place. Can you hear anything different? Are your ears ringing? Is there a smell? If not, you might want to light some sage or other incense. When your eyes are closed, do you see anything? Can you sense anything going on in your chakra centers? The idea here is to open all of your physical, emotional and mental senses to better relate to the spiritual.

Power centers have warm spots. When you are convinced that you are on a crossing of two or more energy leys, run your hand, palm downwards, up and down. I find that somewhere between my hips and my knees there is a warmer spot. This is especially easy to feel in colder weather.

Aquarian Ceremony

Now that you've identified the power center, what do you do there? From here on it's up to you. You now have to take responsibility for your own spiritual growth. No one else can do this for you. Draw on your path so far. Is there a spiritual tradition that is right for you? Use it. You might want to light a candle, to meditate, to read a holy book, the I Ching, or tarot, to chant, to dance, to pray, to make love, to cry, or to heal. It *is* up to you.

For some, words that describe practices designed to enhance spiritual awareness have an empty ring to them – even a negative connotation. Words like "ritual" and "ceremony" bring back for many of us feelings of empty theatre, vestigial movements enacted by spiritually asleep patriarchs who have forgotten the true meaning and spiritual import of many of their ritual actions — dinosaurs in a time when so many have lost their faith/their way. Some are turning back to the Earth to find meaning in their lives and true spiritual awareness and growth. If we, as students of the Earth Mysteries, are to honor these ancient sacred places, and use their energies to enhance the possibility of opening up spiritually ourselves, what should we do when we get there?

Two quick answers are to start by honoring the place — burn sage or other incense, bring a small gift of tobacco or perhaps a pebble from some other sacred site — and meditate. A good way to tune in. But what if there's more than one of you? How can you celebrate together? How does a group of Earth Mystery folks go about doing ceremony? If you're all of the same faith it's a bit simpler, but what if there are different faiths, creeds and religions represented among the people there? How can groups create ceremony that meets the diverse needs of all the people who are involved?

This is an issue that I have been particularly struggling with during my time here in Glastonbury. If I had to describe myself spiritually, I would say that I am a gnostic. (Greek *gnostikos* to know). I feel that as far as my spiritual path is concerned, the buck stops with me. I intend to take personal responsibility for my own spiritual growth. I am not giving that responsibility to someone else. The interesting point here is that if I demand that right for myself, I must also honor that right in everyone else — as long as it isn't harmful to others. This sounds like spiritual anarchy. How then can we create new ceremony using the best of the old and doing it in such a way that all are empowered by the event, and all can participate equally?

We haven't been taught to do it that way. We're trained to be passive in so many ways in both our physical and spiritual lives. In school, it doesn't pay to be creative. Sit in straight lines and give the answer the teacher wants to hear. In church, the priest/minister does it for us. TV. Voter apathy. Western Man has set it up to encourage and reward non-involvement. But what about those of us who do want to be actively involved in our spiritual growth? How can we work together to create a whole that is greater than the sum of its parts? The following is only a suggested process that has been developing at the Glastonbury Earth Mystery Gatherings over the last few years. It is a process that ensures that every participant will have a part in both the design and implementation of the ceremonial event.

The Talking Stick

The talking stick is one tool we use. Also known as the kiva method, everyone sits in a circle (with the power center in the middle if possible as was the case in the circular underground kivas, holy places, of the Anasazi and Hopi). With ongoing groups, a convenor is chosen as the last order of business at the prior meeting. In any event someone calls the group together by picking up the talking stick — it can be anything that can be easily passed from person to person. The person holding the stick is the only one who may talk. As long as s/he has it s/he may laugh, cry, bring up a problem, sing a song, sit quietly, or do anything else. S/he holds the groups' focus until the stick is passed to the next person in the circle. The stick goes all the way around the circle. If someone doesn't want to say anything, they can just pass it on when they get it. Others may speak if recognized by the person holding the stick, but they may only address the specific issue.

No one has the right to say, "Speak up!" Some folks speak in groups more easily than others. By yelling, "Louder!" at someone who is just making their first tentative try at speaking in a group, the reaction is naturally to withdraw. If we're learning to tune in to each other, to build a group Soul, we each have the right to put into the pot what we feel is appropriate, at the volume we feel is appropriate. If you can't hear, find a different way to tune in to that person. What is their body language saying? Can you gain a sense of what they're feeling? The talking stick is a tool that helps us learn how to listen — sometimes in new and unexpected ways.

Decisions are by consensus, and anyone may call for a vote anytime they have the stick. Thumbs up, "yes", thumbs down, "no". If the decision isn't unanimous, only those who voted in the minority get to say why they voted as they did. Then you vote again. If consensus still hasn't been reached, you can either come to the conclusion that the group mind isn't ready to make a decision yet, and postpone that decision until your next meeting, or if it is necessary you can decide to continue to hash it out at that time. In which case, the talking stick continues its way around, starting with the person after the one who called for the vote.

The talking stick is normally a leaderless mode of operation; however, for specific periods of time, for specific tasks, someone can be temporarily appointed as a leader. For example, if money needs to be raised for a group-supported project, and someone is particularly skilled or interested in doing that, s/he is temporarily appointed as fund-raising leader. But normally, there are no leaders, just as there aren't priests in charge. We're all leaders, we're all priestesses/priests.

Talking sticks don't have to be sticks. They can be any object that feels right. I've used a paleolithic hand axe, and have some friends who use a copy of the Willendorf Venus as their talking stick. There's a group in London who use a hat as a talking stick which is passed from head to head. (They can rightly claim that all the best thinking in that group takes place right under that hat!) The groups' choice of their talking stick itself is an interesting process. If your ceremonial group is going to meet on an ongoing basis, each participant brings something that they think would be a good talking stick to the second meeting. At that meeting, everyone, in turn, shows their proposed talking stick to the group, and tells why they think it would make a good one. It is passed around, so everyone can handle it, feel it. After everyone has shared their talking stick, they are once again all passed around. Anyone may place any object outside the circle, no questions asked. The objects keep going around, from hand to hand, until there is only one left inside the circle. This is the group's talking stick. The person who brought it is responsible for bringing it each time the group gets together.

The last order of business is to agree on the time and place of the next meeting, and to choose a convenor for that meeting. That person will hold the talking stick first.

This use of a talking stick isn't always desirable. There are times when a freer form of giving and taking is more appropriate. At that time, the stick is put in the middle; however, anyone can go to the center and pick up the stick any time they want to. At that point the rest of the group must listen to them until they put the stick back into the center. This whole process builds group trust. Sure you can hold the stick as long as you want to, but one quickly feels a sense of how long one can "use up the groups' time." In actual practice, there are very few who hog the stick. And those few who do need that attention at that point anyway. Usually the exact opposite is the result, and a sense of group rather than individual identity is built.

The talking stick is a good way for a group to build its own ceremony, but it has been found equally effective in any group problem solving exercise from designing a more aerodynamic automobile to setting up an Earth Mysteries event.

Ceremony

Ceremony needs to be relevant to the needs of the participants, to the time of year, to the place, and to any other variables that seem important to the group. While ceremonies need to be quite flexible to meet the needs of the Spirit at any given moment, it is fair to say that ceremonies do have a beginning, middle, and end.

One way of being more specific about how ceremonies are divided up could be the following:

1. PURIFICATION: Both the participants and the area to be used for the ceremony need to be cleansed of impurities. When working with spiritual realms, energies that could hamper the successful connection with the groups' goal must be banished, or at least held at bay. Also, the sacred space itself must be delineated, the boundary set.

As far as the purification of individual participants is concerned there are many different ways of doing it. Start by asking, "Are there any methods in my own spiritual background that might accomplish this?" Remember, there is no right way. Of course the ritual bath comes to mind, but I suspect that this might be a bit extreme on most occasions! (Although individual participants might choose to do this at home before they come as a way of initial preparation.) Native Americans use a feather to brush down the aura and to sweep away bits of psycho/ spiritual trash. Incense is used by many different spiritual paths as a way of cleansing the aura. The fragrance of sandalwood joss sticks of the Hindus, Catholic censers billowing frankincense, and the almost addictive aroma of Native American sage burning in an abalone shell come to mind.

To purify the area itself, you might consider taking incense around the perimeter of the site to delineate the sacred space. Some Native Americans honor the four directions East, South, West, and North with burning sage. At each point, they state what that direction means to them. Another way would be to have a guided meditation where each participant imagines a small white ball of love and light at the power center in the center of the circle. It expands outward, sweeping impurities away, until it is totally outside of the sacred and now protected space. Actually just walking around the boundary delineates it. It is the focusing of the intent to purify that is important here, not how the purification is accomplished.

2. INVOCATION: This is the part of the ceremony when the group consciously manifests its intent to connect with the spiritual realms. This can take the form of acknowledging your Creator and asking for

Her/His help in connecting up. It might be the lighting of a fire or a candle in the center of the circle. Once again, the intent to hook up here is what's important, not the form. If the group shares a common deity or Avatar - The Great Spirit, Jesus, Krishna, the Great Mother, Buddah, or Gaia, the Earth Mother — S/He can be invoked. The point is to connect to the spiritual in a mutually agreeable way so that each participant can feel for her/himself the reality of these realms.

3. RECEIVING: A time of slowly building the energy. It can be done with chanting, moving in place, simple repetitive songs, dancing, making a human chain that snakes into a tight spiral and then out again, drums, pipes, rattles, hand clapping. Slowly the pace is picked up until it reaches a certain pitch, and then it falls. But it picks up again and goes even higher. And down again. Then even higher still. It's a rising spiritual orgasm. All are free to express their feelings and awarenesses in ways that they choose. The important thing here is that contact has been made.

4. GIVING: The energy that has been built up can now be used in many healing ways to further potentize the site itself, to send thoughts of peace to a troubled world, to see the healing light surrounding friends who are in need. Or it can be given back to the Sky and/or the Earth. In a sense, this giving earths the energy and helps to bring the participants back safely.

Another thing that you can do is to end the ceremony with a light meal. Bread, water from the local holy well, wine, and pomegranates are some of the foods that I have seen used at this time. They further help to ground the participants.

I can just hear some saying, "Yeah, but this could be dangerous. You could get in over your head. Fools rush in ... etc., etc." The saving grace here is the group itself. The group wisdom will keep the ceremony within bounds. If ten or a hundred people get together to do ceremony at a sacred site, you can be sure that some of them have done it before, and they know some of the way and the pitfalls — if any. The talking stick and consensus assures that those who have been there before will be able to warn the group if the novices are getting in over their heads. Dowsing is a good tool to use when in doubt here. Western Man brought us up to not really believe in the spiritual — oh, give it lip service for sure — so this is a new world for many. Like spiritual pioneers.

The new frontier.

Another thought. If the Giving stage doesn't happen, some participants might have some difficulty in getting back home to their bodies. Rescue Remedy, a combination of several of the Bach Flower Remedies, works well. These remedies are designed to work on the emotional and higher levels rather than physical. Just a drop or two on the tongue can be of great help in any emergency situation. These Remedies will be discussed further in the section on Dowsing and Healing.

Purification, Invocation, Receiving, Giving, one path to an effective ceremony. Please remember that *there is no right way to do ceremony.* No right order. But let's take the four above steps as an example. In the planning/discussion stage of the ceremony, each of these four steps can be discussed separately, and those with particular skills can know in advance roughly when it will be appropriate for them to make those contributions. Don't get hung up on minute details. Leave room for the Spirit to move you. When everyone then understands why they are doing a particular ceremony, the steps become clear, and each knows when what they have to offer is best done. In the Old Age, we hired/appointed Priests to do it for us. Now we are all priests and priestesses taking responsibility for our own spiritual growth, and working together to help each other grow.

Yes, there are beautiful rituals from many spiritual paths that could be used and followed verbatim, but I prefer to pick and choose, to be part of a process in which we build our own ceremony using good parts from several different traditions.

You can lead a horse to water (an interesting analogy), but you can't make him drink. Each of us must decide for ourselves what we will do in sacred space, how we will use it. Herstory has show that Western Man hasn't done so well. It is up to us as spiritual dowsers to help turn things around. Each one of us, going to our own power centers all over this Mother of ours intent on spiritual growth, can play an important part. Help us all by helping yourself.

I do not seek to follow
in the footsteps
of the wo/men of old.

I seek
what
they sought.

Dowsing and Healing

Water-witching was the only kind of dowsing that was allowed to survive the witchcraft persecutions. It was just too valuable, too crucial to the lives of all of us, to be suppressed. The Age of Rationalism finally quenched the religious frenzy to totally eradicate those on the spiritual path who thought for themselves. By the middle of the twentieth century, dowsing could be seen by Western Man as something that was merely "quaint" and non-threatening. Most of us associated dowsing, if we had heard of it at all, with something practiced out in the country by eccentric old men who thought they could find the site of a water well by using a forked apple branch. Water was all we knew, all they knew. It was a small group of male water dowsers, for example, who started the American Society of Dowsers in 1961 as quaint entertainment to lure the tourists to the colorful Northeast Kingdom of Vermont countryside at the peak of the fall foliage season.

In the last ten years however, there has been an explosion of interest in other areas of dowsing as well. If one can judge by the attendance at workshops at the Annual Convention of the ASD held in Danville, Vermont each September, the vast majority of members are now involved in this ancient art because of their interest in healing. This is the area of dowsing that is most immediately useful to most people. How often are city dwellers called upon to dowse a well for drinking water? Never – or at least the exception would prove the rule. What else is there for the urban dowser to do? In European cities there are old churches built on power centers that are interesting to dowse, and even many U.S. city parks have power centers (Central Park in New York City is a fine example). But it is healing and health that has the attention of most dowsers today.

In traditional Liberal Arts fashion, American dowsers have tended to compartmentalize healing (Health) as something different and separate from the Earth Energies. As a result, most beginning dowsers think that they are totally unrelated subjects. The connection between power centers like Lourdes and healing is forgotten. But healing is one of the major attributes of sacred space, and many dowsers on the spiritual path are beginning to see both the Earth Energies and healing as part of the same package.

Permission

Before considering the healing process itself, let us consider two very important notions. The first is one that is totally ignored by many dowsers: the necessity of permission. I've chosen to limit myself by requiring that the person being healed give conscious permission for me to intervene. If the person is too ill to give permission, it can be given by a close relative. Permission is the link, the thread that connects the dowser to the person in need of help. You don't have to spell out all of the details of what you intend to do in order to secure permission. What is important is that you speak to the person to be healed on the level that they can hear. It is reasonable to assume that many would be put off by, "Will you give me permission to neutralize the noxious veins in your house and to get rid of several rather nasty ghosties and ghoulies that seem to be hanging on you at the moment?" That's really not on. For some, all one needs to say is, "May I pray for you?" Others will need, and be open to, a deeper discussion of what you are offering, but in any event, get permission. You wouldn't go into someone's house without their consent. Why should you attempt to work with the energies in and around their bodies without their permission as well?

Ego

A second word of caution. Your ego can very easily get you into trouble here. If you think that *you* are doing the healing, there is a chance that you will function much like a battery. The healing energy will flow from you to the other person. But batteries go dead. Sooner or later this depletion of your life force will put your own health in jeopardy.

It's better to think of oneself as a channel for the healing energies. You're just the middle wo/man. The energies come from the highest source you can imagine. They can either flow in through your feet, or through your head, and out through your hands or whatever part of your body you use to focus these energies. Offer yourself as a channel, a part of the flow, not as a battery (the Source).

Gathering Information

The seven levels of dowsing ability continue to be a good model in terms of dowsing and healing. As the first four levels are purely informational, they would relate to diagnostic skills. Dowsers have known for years that the pendulum is a fine tool for checking out various foods to see if they will be adversely effected by them. Pendulums are very effective in working with allergies, and may be used to determine the sex of unborn babies (as well as how much the baby will weigh and the date of birth). Speaking of birth dates, if that information is not available, dowsing is a fine way to determine your own exact time of birth for astrological birth charts. All these applications involve informational dowsing, and you can get the answer to practically any health question that you can think of. You don't need a radionics box or a medical degree; all you need is the right question and some dowsing skill.

Auras

In many instances, disease can be seen on higher metaphysical planes before they manifest themselves on the physical. A good example would be the man whose boss is really pushing him to meet impossible sales goals, who then drives home through massive rush hour traffic jams to find his wife has also had a hard day, and his son has just

Hole in the Aura

wrecked his motorcycle, etc. These emotional overloads will be visible on the astral or emotional body long before they manifest as ulcers down on the physical. They lend themselves nicely to discovery by the dowser as holes, or weak spots, in a person's health aura.

> Try looking for these holes with a single L rod. Find a willing subject, and dowse the edge of her/his astral or emotional body. The rods will deflect at the proper spot as you approach your friend's physical body (I find the edge at two-and-a-half to three feet out). Now hold the L rod parallel to the body and run it up and down at that distance out. If you come to a hole, the L rod will swing in towards the body. Remember, this will show emotional problems, not physical ones.
>
> This same technique can be used to identify problems on the physical plane as well. Focus your intent down on the physical. Run your L rod up and down the body. At places where it swings in, there will be a scar of an old injury, a present problem that s/he is aware of, or one that is there, but s/he is not aware of yet.

Map Dowsing

Map dowsing works just as well here. Draw an outline of a body.

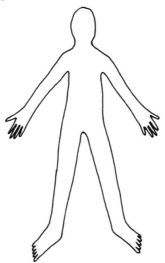

Name _____

Write the name of the person you intend to dowse below the outline to focus your intent on who it is you're dowsing. Use a pendulum, and say to yourself, "I want to look for medical imbalances in so and so's body. Can I? May I? (Have you actually asked their permission to do this?) Am I ready?" If you get all affirmatives, with your pendulum in the search position, run your finger down the figure starting at the top of the head. Where there's a problem, the pendulum will go out of the search position into some other pattern. My pendulum goes from the search position (for me, back and forth) into either a clockwise (yang) direction or in a counterclockwise (yin) direction. This describes the kind of energy my pendulum is over. It gives me a clue as to what the imbalance is – too much yin or too much yang.

I have to say that these techniques are potentially one half parlor tricks (I'm not into them), and one half speculative at best. When one gets reactions at points where the subject can not relate to any problem, it is often assumed that dowsing just doesn't work. That could actually be the case, but perhaps you as a dowser can't function on the level necessary to get accurate results here (as is so often true at parties when dowsing is trucked out as something a bit weird). So they're just spurious readings. On the other hand, it could be that you have picked up a problem of which the subject is not yet aware. Remember to be very care-full in speaking with someone about what you think you may have found. Your silence may well be as frightening as blurting out some dreadful finding.

In any case, the answers aren't particularly relevant to the kinds of healing that I have been involved with. You don't need to know what the specific problem is to be a channel for balancing the other person. The healer does not need to be aware of the diagnosis to be a channel for healing.

Dowsing and the Astral Body:
The Bach Flower Remedies

Edward Bach, a British physician, gave up his lucrative Harley Street practice in 1930 to devote his full-time to developing carefully prepared essences of some thirty-eight flowers which he found to be effective in treating imbalances on the emotional and mental planes. These essences are available in separate small bottles with droppers and are added to water in homeopathic doses.

Many ways of selecting which of these emotional balancers to use
have been developed over the years, and dowsing can be a very useful
tool in this process. The Bach Centre has a little basic hand-out called,
appropriately enough, "Bach Flower Remedies". Aside from being a
quick and informative discussion of the history and use of the Remedies,
and addresses in various parts of the world where you can get the
Remedies themselves, the back page is an excellent list of the thirty-
eight basic Remedies and Rescue Remedy, an especially useful combination of several Remedies, with a brief statement concerning the area of
the emotions or attitudes that each remedy is good for. Rescue Remedy
is an absolute must in any first aid kit. A combination of several of the
Bach Flower Remedies (Cherry Plum, Clematis, Impatiens, Rock Rose
and Star of Bethlehem), Rescue Remedy is good for shock, small children
who are crying incoherently, jet lag, drug induced freak outs, extreme
fear bordering on terror, difficulty in returning from higher planes, and
many other emergency situations where shock is a factor.

I've found the Bach list to be a very effective tool in working with
people and problems. Let's say that things aren't going too well
for you at some point. Pull out the list, read through it, and try to
identify with one of the Remedies. Among the list of Remedies,
some are good to help you out of depression, others assist in
times of heavy change, indifference and for when you really feel
the need to cleanse yourself. There are many others as well. Try to
pick the one that most closely reflects your outlook towards the
problem you are dealing with. You might have to settle for two
because you can't decide between them which is more
important, but if you can, try for just one.

Now it's time for the pendulum work. "I want to find out
intuitively which Remedy is most appropriate for me now. Can I?
May I? Am I ready?"

You could work your way through all thirty-eight one bottle at a
time, "Is this the one?", but that's deadly. It just takes too long,
and gives your Western Man consciousness too much time to
intrude. If you get them from the Bach Centre, the Remedies will
come in four white boxes. Hold one of the boxes in your hand (I
also make sure that I don't even know which box I'm holding), "Is
one of these the most appropriate for me now?" Do that until you
find the right box. Then you can put your finger-tips on the top of
the first four bottles and so on until you find the most appropriate
Remedy.

Get the bottle out that you've dowsed and hold it in your

hand. "Is this the right one?" If so, look at the Remedy you've chosen and read the emotional/attitudinal issues associated with it. If you can easily relate to the one you dowsed, great! If you can't, it's probably something that's even more important for you to work with.

Now find out how many drops of each you will need to put in your specific remedy. You will need a clean bottle with a dropper. You can get them at your local drug store/chemist. As I'm living in Glastonbury, I use Chalice Well water as the solution into which the various remedies go. I am aware that some feel that Chalice Well water is already the equivalent to the Bach Remedy called Rock Water. I feel that the healing potential of the Chalice Well water itself outweighs this consideration. If you have a holy well near you, by all means use it. Any spring or well water that is good to drink will work fine.

You will find that you need to use from one to five drops of Remedy in your solution. Hold each essence in your hand and ask, "Do I need more than one drop of this? More than two?" And so on until you find out the number of drops for each Remedy. As you put the drops in, say to yourself what those specific drops are for. Put your intent into that bottle as you shake it to mix the Remedies into the solution.

Dowse how many times a day (usually two or three) you should take them, how many drops each time, and the length of time to be taking them. I usually make a little label with key words on it that will help me to focus my intent each time, and dosage information. Each time you take the drops, say to yourself those key words. They re-focus your intent to heal yourself.

I find that these flower essences work homeopathically in that the less you use, the more powerful they are. We're not working on the physical level of "I've got a stomach ache," but on the emotional one of "I'm so scared of speaking in public that I won't do it, even though I know that I have some important things to say."

In Western Man America it's "More is better." On the emotional level, it's the mirror opposite. "Less is more." Homeopathy works on this principle in that the healing substances are mixed with water (secussed) until at times there is some doubt if there is even a molecule of the initial substance left in solution. This makes homeopathic medicine more powerful, and more capable of operating on more subtle levels. The Bach Flower Remedies work like this as well.

The beautiful thing about choosing one Remedy analytically and one

intuitively is that you are treating yourself using both ways of
functioning. It's really a wholistic approach.

Higher Level Dowsing/Healing

The Bach Flower Remedies are an appropriate response to the information gathered in one of the first four levels of dowsing; however, to be
a channel for healing involves operating at the fifth and sixth levels of
dowsing where the dowser/healer can go and change things (stop the
cancer) or cause *new* forms of manifestation (creating new cells in the
lung to replace damaged tissue). Levels five and six are open to many on
the path, but I've never met anyone who operates on the seventh level
– someone who was so evolved that their will and the Creator's were
one. I suspect that there have been very few who have walked this Earth
who have operated at that level, and they were the Avatars who
brought us the world's great religions.

For me, healing ultimately boils down to prayer. Somehow you must
connect yourself with the Infinite and bring that power down to bring
about balance within the person to be healed. Some use the channel of
faith. Others who have consciously experienced the spiritual realms just
know how to connect up. They've been through that door before, so
they know where it is. It doesn't make any difference how one makes the
connection; there are many paths up the mountain, but they all lead to
the top.

I had a teacher once who said the only thing that we have a right to
ask of our Maker is to be consciously closer. This is the path of the
mystic. Plug in to the energy and go in (or up, or out).

Healers, though, need to do something slightly different. They still
need to plug in to the Source, but they are interested in manifesting that
energy down on the physical, emotional, mental, or spiritual planes,
bringing balance to a situation. It is the intent of the healer to be a
channel that focuses that power.

Filling Holes in the Aura

Many chiropractors compare the length of their patient's legs to judge if
their adjustments have been effective. I prefer to use the arms for this
purpose because it is easier for the patient her/himself to get a sense of
her/his state of balance. Before-and-after checks give us both a sense of
what is going on.

> Have your friend lie on her/his back on the floor. Kneel above
> her/his head and take their hands placing your thumbs in their

palms. Gently stretching her/his arms outwards and upwards, bringing them so that they are flat on the floor, in line with the spine, stretched above her/his head as far as they can comfortably go. Bring the thumbnails of both hands together. The vast majority of the time, one arm will be slightly shorter than the other. You can see it, and your friend can feel this if s/he rubs the tip of the thumbnail of her/his shorter arm against the thumb of the longer one, thus s/he can feel a symptom of her/his own imbalance.

Before beginning any healing work, take a moment to hook up to the Great Spirit, God, Goddess, Allah, The One, or whatever you call Her/Him. Holding both of your friend's hands in yours, ask to be a channel of healing. Know that this is to be.

Then ask your friend to roll over on her/his stomach. Move to your friend's side and, with your pendulum in the search position, say, "I want to look for holes in the health aura. May I? Can I? Am I ready?" Put your free hand at the top of her/his spine at the point where it reaches the neck. There is a particularly large bone there, the seventh cervical vertebra. Slowly run your finger, bone by bone, down their spine towards the tail bone, or coccyx. At least one point on your journey, the pendulum will probably go from your search position to some other movement. Whatever the signal, when your pendulum alters its movement, there is a hole that begins at that point. The pendulum will continue to rotate that way until your finger is at the other side of the hole, and then, as you continue downwards, it will go back into the search position. In all the times I have done this, I have only seen one person who didn't have at least one hole.

Most people have a two- or three-inch hole around the small of their back. At times it can be even larger than this. Some people have other smaller holes above that one, or below it, though that is less common. Remember where the holes are. Let your friend know where they are by touching them on their back at those places. When you get to the coccyx, stop.

Polarity of Fingers

Before we do anything to deal with these holes, we have to take a minute and look at our fingers as tools of healing. My dowsing indicates that the polarity changes from the tip of one finger to another. Hold your pendulum over each of the fingers of your free hand, and ask for the polarity. I find my left index finger to be yin (or minus), the middle yang (or plus), the third yin and the fourth yang. What do you find?

Yin is receptive; it seems to take things in like a vacuum cleaner. Yang is out-going. Put the tip of a yin finger of your free hand on the center of the highest hole in the spine. When I do this, the pendulum starts going counterclockwise, my yin or "no" response.

Like a vacuum cleaner, I can feel tingling run up my arm as the negativity flows out of the other person into me. Here's where the notion of being a channel becomes important. When I feel that tingling going up my arm, I "see" it continuing up my neck, and out of the top of my head. I give it to the Universe. You can also "see" it going down your body and out of your feet to the Earth. Either way is fine. If you see yourself as a battery, that negativity will stay inside you. The person to be healed may get a healing, but you get her/his problem. That's not a fair trade.

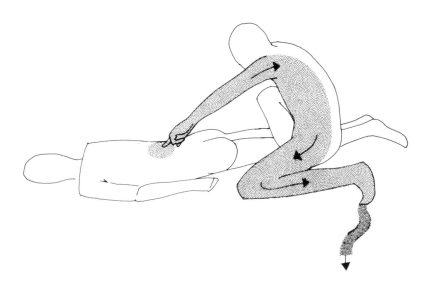

Continue holding your yin finger on that spot until the pendulum goes back to your search position. Then put your yang finger on the same point to channel healing energies in. This time the tingling goes the other way, down your arm. The pendulum will be giving you your "yes", or yang, response. You will notice that the pendulum rotates in your yang response for about the same number of rotations as the earlier yin response.

Healing energies are flowing from the Cosmos, through you, into your friend, replacing the negativity that has just flowed out through you. Just as with the blood in our circulatory system, the life force system also delivers the spiritual nutrients and picks up the psychic and emotional garbage.

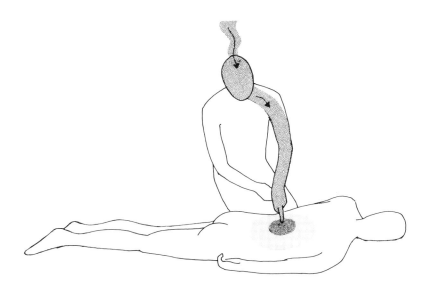

Go back to your yin finger, and start the process again. You will notice that each pair of yin and yang responses is shorter in the number of rotations of the pendulum than the previous pair was. Continue this until you get only the search position with both the yin and yang fingers.

   Get your friend to help in this process. Explain what you are
doing, and when your yin finger is on her/his back, say, "out".
Your friend can focus on that point in their back and release,
imagining darkness, pain and anger flowing to that point and out
your finger. Then, "in". This time s/he imagines healing light and
love are flowing in at that point filling her/him with peace and
balance. It's a cooperative process. Go on down the back, and
repair all of the holes. This back and forth, cleaning out and filling
in, feels like the tide.

> *We are the flow,*
> *We are the ebb,*
> *We are the weaver,*
> *We are the web.*

Check the back once more when you have finished. The
pendulum should stay in the search position from the seventh
cervical vertebra down to the coccyx. Have your friend roll over
on her/his back and check the length of the arms again. In most
cases, the tips of the nails of the thumbs are together. Your friend
can feel that balance on the physical level for her/himself. The
final thing to do is to verbally give thanks for what has been done.
It is a way of closing the healing session and thanking your Creator
for allowing you to be a channel for Her/His healing energy.

While specific injured areas can perhaps use more special attention, this
seems to be a quick way to balance out the entire system. Most healing
doesn't need to take a long time. If it's going to work, it does.

Incidentally, there is an even quicker method of doing this than the
two-finger-back-and-forth method we've just discussed. After determining where the holes are (actually, you don't even have to do that), place
your first three fingers of one of your hands on your friend's tail bone —
the middle finger in the center and a finger on either side. Run up the
back bone to the seventh cervical vertebra imagining that you are
zipping the spine up and closing and filling all the holes. It feels like
closing a zip lock plastic sandwich bag. While this technique is much
quicker, I urge you to use the two-finger-back-and-forth method until
you know that you can competently channel healing energy in both
directions. It is a useful skill.

Balancing the Chakras
The pendulum is also effective as a tool to tune up the chakras.

Normally, I am really suspicious of "special" dowsing tools – the ball-bearing mounted, platinum coated, witness chambered, auto-antenna extending L rod (only $400.00!), and huge crystal pendulums in expensive silver and gold settings come to mind. Baloney! This just appeals to the decadent end of the old age and its notion that the more something costs, the better it is. When one is using dowsing to seek information, what the tool is made out of doesn't make a bit of difference unless you choose to limit yourself by thinking that it does. I've made a very effective pendulum out of a small rock and a dandelion stem. If you take the attitude that anything can work, you will always be able to find a dowsing device when you need it. White pine needles make really good Y rods. I'd like to have a penny for every coat hanger that has been bent into an L rod. Lots of people use a ring on a string for a pendulum. When doing informational dowsing, it doesn't make any difference what the tool is made of as long as it's reasonably balanced. Ultimately the idea is to get rid of the tool anyway.

On the other hand, on fifth and sixth levels where one uses dowsing to send energy out, the use of a crystal may help focus that intent. A good example can be seen in the following technique to balance the chakras. I do use a quartz crystal pendulum for this work. I must admit to some trepidation here because ultimately we don't need any tools other than our bodies to do any of this, and I don't want you to feel that you *must* have a quartz crystal pendulum or it won't work. But I have found that they do seem to enhance the process. Crystals are not toys. If you haven't already worked with them, and are not familiar with how to clean and program them, perhaps you might consider skipping the following exercise until you become more knowledgeable concerning crystals. If in doubt, ask your pendulum.

> Have a friend lie on her/his back on the floor. You can do the arm length test if you want. Again, take time to tune in to your Creator. Be clear about your intent here. You want to balance and bring into harmony your friend's chakras. "I want to balance my friend's chakras. Can I? May I? Am I ready?"
>
> Hold your pendulum over their root chakra. You remember from the last time we dowsed the chakras that the root chakras of women have a yin polarity, men have a yang polarity and that this alternates as you go up. Let's say your friend is a woman. When you hold it over her root chakra, your pendulum will go from the search position into your yin response, and continue to rotate in that direction for awhile. It will then go back into the search position. That means that point has had enough. Go up the spine

until you come to the second chakra. The pendulum will go from
your search position into your yang response when you are over
it. Stay there until it goes back into the search position, and so on
up to the top. If for some reason, the pendulum just stays in the
search position over any particular chakra, skip it, and go
immediately on to the next. For whatever reason, it isn't to be
worked with at that time.

Again, I feel that I must say that you don't need a quartz crystal
pendulum to do this. Any weight on a string will work; however, it does
seem to me that when I transmit rather than receive, crystal quartz helps
focus the intent.

Healing and Western Man's Law

In Britain, there is a much more open climate to alternative forms of
healing. Alternate medicine has no accountability to allopathic (read:
Western Man's) medicine. There have been several attempts by MDs to
take over alternative medicine, but it has been put down each time on
the grounds that MDs, allopaths, are of a different tradition and
therefore don't have the tools to understand/sit in judgment on
alternative medicine. At the Glastonbury Natural Health Centre for
example there are people doing acupuncture, medical herbalism, counsel-
ling, dietary allergy advice, Osteopathy, massage, Shiatsu, healing,
relaxation techniques, Reiki, Bach Flower Remedies, zero balancing,
reflexology, cancer self-help and tissue salts all without any M.D.'s
supervision. And it's perfectly legal.

In the United States today it's a different story entirely. Allopathic
medicine and the U.S. pharmecutical companies hold an incredible
amount of legal clout. Alternative health care must be done under a
doctor's supervision, and subject to the restrictions of her/his license. It's
perfectly legal to *study* alternative healing techniques and to do
associated research (read: to remain totally objective and uninvolved),
but just don't try actually doing it. There may be some opportunities in
the law's protection of certain practitioners of religious healing, but even
this is risky and needs to be done carefully. The U.S. law in effect says,
"look, but don't touch."

Earth Energies and Healing

All of the above operations can be aided by performing them at power
centers. All forms of spiritual activities are enhanced when done at these

crossings of energy leys and underground domes and veins of primary water. Healing is no exception. Some holy sites are associated specifically with healing, Men-an-tol in Land's End, Cornwall was said to cure scrofulous (tubercular) children and rickets when the subject went three times through the hole against the Sun. Many Irish holy wells are connected with cures for eye ailments. But no matter, if you attempt to heal at a site associated with healing, you also have the support of the belief of the many supplicants who came there before you. Thought has form, and it can work for you. All of this tends to enhance the possibility of a healing actually occurring.

Crawling Widdershins Through Men-an-tol

Earth Energies Detrimental To a Person's Health

When the Earth Mother is by herself, in the form of underground veins of primary water not associated with energy leys, humans can be affected in different ways. Unfortunately, when dowsers first started to explore these zones of apparent negativity in the United States, they called them "noxious zones". This is a yin, or feminine, energy that we are discussing and it really is a put-down of our Earth Mother to call her "noxious". Another problem with this term is that it leads the dowser to assume that such zones are always bad for humans. It wasn't until several years ago that it occurred to me to find out if there could be any beneficial uses of this yin energy. First of all, many animals other than humans love it. Cats and cloven-hoofed animals like cows and deer choose to spend time over these places (remember the deer beds being over a vein of water?) The energy seems to affect them differently than it does us humans.

Many ancient spiritual paths talk about the wheel of life. One side has to do with creation and growth, the other with death and decomposition. In India, the Hindus refer to this as Vishnu, the creator, and Kali, the destroyer. Neither is good nor bad; they're merely points on the wheel, integral parts of the whole circle. Under Kali energy, things fall apart, disintegrate. Underground concentrations of certain minerals, fault lines and underground veins of primary water, especially crossings of these veins, are sources of this Kali energy. Things seem to break down and decompose here more easily. Such a zone would be an excellent place to put your garden's compost pile. I also suspect that there might be some benefit in putting hyperactive children for controlled periods over such places. It might be a way to take out and relieve the pressure of some of their excess energy.

Kali centers are also excellent places to get rid of things. Let's say that you've been angry with your neighbors for the last ten years, and it's gone on long enough. Balance needs to be brought back to the relationship. A transformation is called for. A good place to start is within yourself. Being aware that the anger has indeed gone on long enough is a good beginning, but is there any way to actually get rid of all those negative thoughts that you have generated towards your neighbor over the last ten years? Before you go over to talk with her/him, stand on a crossing of underground veins and give your anger to your Earth Mother. Think of all the wrongs that that person next door has done you and how angry you have felt. Feel those feelings again, and at the same time, consciously give them to the Earth Mother to digest and decompose and use to make something new — as in the new relationship that you intend to have with your neighbor.

Another example. All of us, at one time or another, have received letters that we really don't like, even to the point that we would like to get that energy out of our home entirely. Take the letter to a crossing of veins of primary water and burn it, scattering the ashes over that spot. The Earth Mother will take the energy and help it decompose. I did this once with a letter from a fellow who was particularly obnoxious. A year or so later, I was trying to remember why I had been so angry with him. I simply couldn't. I had given that away, and it was gone. The connection had been broken.

These zones can help you get rid of junk that you don't want or need anymore, things that are getting in the way of your spiritual growth. And don't worry about dumping on your Earth Mother. She chews up that energy, digests it and transforms it into something new and useful. At Kali points, that's her function. She's pleased to be of service, pleased to be tuned in to again.

I've found that thinking about our Earth as a living being helps to shift one's consciousness towards the intuitive. It also helps one to be more aware of the effect of the logging in the Brazilian rain forest, strip mining, oil spills and other environmental disasters. Spiritual ecology is just another term for Earth Mysteries.

Spiritual House-cleaning

Just as sacred spaces like Stonehenge or the Great Pyramid were designed to maximize the energies that were there for spiritual growth, people's homes can be places where the energies are used to enhance love and growth for the family that lives there. Unfortunately, many homesites are affected adversely by various negative thought forms, underground veins of primary water and the degenerative entities they sometimes harbor. Dealing with such things is what some dowsers refer to as "spiritual house-cleaning".

We've suggested a way of erasing the negative thought forms, but how can we deal with these energies that are so detrimental to a person's health that are magnified by underground veins of primary water? We're walking on potentially dangerous ground here. It's one of those times when the, "This is what I want to do. Can I? *May I?* Am I ready?" *is absolutely essential*. If you get a "no" after asking "May I — Do I have permission?", by all means, go no further. This question will protect you from getting in over your head. There are other energies, found in some homes, that take a lot of training to work with safely, and they are beyond the scope of this little book.

I truly dislike the phrase "beyond the scope of this book." It implies a cop-out on my part. But I've felt several times while writing this that I am dancing on the edge of things that could get some of my readers in trouble. It has to do with time. The process from first time dowser to house-cleaner took me over fifteen years. It took me several years from the time I first saw a competent dowser do a full house-cleaning, including helping entities across to the other side, to the time when I felt secure/knowledgeable/skilled enough to actually try it myself. One of the first few times I tried house-cleaning by myself, I got into trouble with entities. They were raising havoc in the house. It wasn't a pleasant experience. I give thanks that I knew a competent dowser who helped me out. The one thing this book can't give you is time. And yet it is time to talk about such things. Some of you will be ready much more quickly than I was, but remember the importance of the question "May I?"

Assuming you got a "yes" for the "May I?" question, there are various ways of dealing with these veins of water. Some can be done by third level dowsers, and some techniques require fifth level dowsing skills.

Diverting Veins

To begin with, it is possible for dowsers to divert veins of water. It all has to do with sound. Builders of highways have found that when they use dynamite to blast through a hill, water wells in the area sometimes go dry. The sonic shock waves of the blast actually knock the veins of water out of the well-head and open new veins! Dowsers have used this knowledge for years to change the direction of a vein of underground water to drive it into a dry well or pond, or to knock it out of a wet basement. It can also be used to knock veins with energies that are detrimental to a person's health out of a house. But let's look at how to move these veins.

Find the vein that you want to move by using on-site, or level number one dowsing. Using "yes" or "no" questions, determine how deep the vein is – it doesn't do any good to divert a vein that's forty feet down into a well that is only thirty-five feet deep, or a vein that's twenty feet down to dry out a wet basement that's only twelve feet deep! "Is it over ten feet down to the center of the vein? Over twenty? etc."

Decide also which way is downstream so you know which direction the vein is flowing. Before you attempt to move the vein, it would also be important to ask if that vein is presently feeding another well, or if for any other reason the vein should not be moved.

Assuming all is fine, locate the exact heart of the vein. This seems to be the critical part. Locate both sides of the vein at the exact point where you intend to divert it. Locate a point half way between the two edges of the vein. "Is this the right place?" At that point, drive a metal crowbar at least a foot to eighteen inches into the ground. Just as you would a croquet ball, strike the side of the crowbar where it meets the Earth, swinging in the direction that you want the vein to go. There appear to be various theories as to how many times to hit it. I ask my pendulum. It's usually between three and eight times. If you've done everything correctly, the vein then flows in the direction you've driven it.

Don't become discouraged if this doesn't work the first time you try this technique. I once went to a dry pond three or four times before I managed to get it right. Even the experts in this kind of dowsing don't always get it right. But it does work a great deal of the time. Remember, you have to dowse *only* for veins that are *above the bottom* of the well, pond or basement. If you knock a vein at sixty feet into a well hole that is only fifty feet deep, it won't do much good. Also, be sure to hit the *exact heart* of the vein with your iron rod.

Earth Acupuncture

This idea of putting an iron rod into a vein of underground water can also be useful in cleaning houses of zones that are detrimental to a person's health without actually having to move the vein. Perhaps the most popular method of doing this is to use two iron rods such as those used in reinforcing concrete. It is about the diameter of your ring finger, and should be cut in pieces twelve to eighteen inches long.

Again, before you begin, ask permission. "This is what I want to do. Can I? **May I?** Am I ready?" If all is "yes", locate a point on the vein about thirty feet before it enters the house. Find the exact center of the vein, and drive the rod into the Earth, making sure that it is several inches below the surface so it won't mess up your lawn mower. (Some dowsers like to check the polarity of the iron rod first. "Show me the polarity of this end." They put the yin end into the Earth, and drive the yang end with the hammer.) In any event, next go to the point on the other side of the house where the same vein exits, and again, about thirty feet out, drive the other rod into the heart of the vein. You will find that the Earth Energies that had emanated from the vein between those two points have been neutralized.

Notice the language that I've been using, "Drive a metal rod into the heart of the vein." For me this brings up the image of killing a vampire. In a real sense these veins *are* psychic vampires. They seem to suck the life force out of us, and thereby make us less able to combat disease, less healthy, less whole. If you used muscle testing to test the energies before you began, your friend will now test strong, and her/his aura will not contract when standing on the vein between these two iron rods.

Why iron? For one thing, it appears to be a metal that has an interesting effect on the Earth Energies. Many myths speak of the time when we first were discovering the use of metals. Shamans, or Medicine Men were the first smiths. They knew of iron's ability to cause these energies to deviate from their natural path, just as it can cause a needle on a compass to deviate from magnetic north.

Iron was not used in the construction of Solomon's Temple. "When the house was built, it was with stone prepared at the quarry; so that neither hammer nor axe nor any tool of iron was heard in the temple, while it was being built." (I Kings 6:7) On the other hand, the troughs and pools at the Chalice Well in Glastonbury are stained red because the (chalybeate) water is so full of iron. That well is famous for her healing power. Iron seems to affect the Earth Energies in ways that we are only beginning to rediscover.

Mental Diversion

It is also possible to move these veins mentally. This would be an example of level five dowsing, going there for information, but also being able to effect changes there as well. Stopping the cancer. Moving the vein. I had a good experience of that in 1981 when I visited a friend in western New York. Her home was full of veins of water, which we neutralized. At that time, as much of the water out there does, her well water tasted like a cross between sulphur and iron.

After my return home to Vermont, I received a letter from my friend who wrote that three days after I had been there (enough time to use up all of the reserve water in her holding tank), her water changed from sulphur/iron to a very strong iodine flavor, and was there anything further that I might do?

Deciding to try map dowsing, I used a blank page in my journal, and put a dot on the page that represented her well-head. I then used my pendulum to find out where the veins were. Two were crossing right at the well-head. One produced nine gallons a minute, and was good potable (drinkable) water. The other was only four gallons a minute, and it was the vein that carried the iodine. I asked for help from the local water spirit to move the smaller vein so that it would miss the well. I remember that I had the two veins marked on the paper, and all of a sudden I "saw" a yellowish-green line bend out to the south, from the point just before the iodine vein entered the well-head, and loop around the well to rejoin the vein on the other side.

About a month later, I got a letter from my friend who said, "I really appreciate the change in the water from *sulphur* to *iodine* to *good*!! It also seems *not* to make any calcium deposit (like boiler scale) in the tea kettle. What a change."

Once again — it might be sounding like a broken record — before you try to neutralize or move any veins running under your house, *please* ask, "May I do this?" and then just to be sure ask, "Is this the truth?" I know that you might be really excited to work with these energies, so excited that you really want a "yes" answer. Be really clear with yourself that while you are waiting for an answer, instead of saying to yourself, "I hope it's 'yes'," it's, "I wonder what the answer will be?" There are life forms that live off that negative energy, and if they are there, and you remove the veins, they will start living off you instead. Getting a "no" when you ask "May I?" could indicate the presence of "ghosties and ghoulies and things that go bump in the night." If non-physical entities are present, please don't remove or neutralize the veins! It's time for you to link up with a dowser who has had some experience with these matters. But there are other ways to deal with these veins.

If your bed is over a crossing of veins, move your bed. If your favorite chair where you sit when you watch TV is over a crossing, move the chair. Please don't stake the veins around your home if you get a "no" at any point when you go through the "This is what I want to do. Can I? *May I?* Am I ready?"

It is true that one of the beauties of dowsing is that it requires both analytical and intuitive faculties; however, I have found that this process of asking the question, and then waiting for the tool to react can ultimately retard spiritual growth. I suspect that if you polled a bunch of really good dowsers, you would find that they spend nine-tenths of their time asking the right question. In our art, this is critical. You don't ask, "Where's the nearest water?", you say something like, "Where is the nearest vein of drinkable water that has a year 'round flow of over five gallons a minute, and is less than twenty feet down." Then as you turn around to scan the area, for a brief moment, you switch from analytical to intuitive, from physical to spiritual. When you see, or maybe feel the rod going down, you know the best place to dig is in that direction.

The problem here is that if you are intent on opening up to the spiritual, and growing in the Light, you can use dowsing to determine that these realms are indeed real, but you can't actually experience them directly. A dowser's consciousness stays in the physical while s/he waits for the answer, and, as the rod goes down, it is her/his physical senses (sight and touch) that let her/him know the answer. Dowsing is a good bridge. But it is only a bridge.

This is why I've said from the beginning of this book that the ultimate goal of the spiritual dowser is to get rid of the tools. Tools keep you in duality rather than seeing it all as one. Practice deviceless dowsing. And yes, while it's fine to "see" a pendulum moving on the screen of your third eye, why not go for "seeing" the spot in the field where it's best to dig? Maybe your eyes will be drawn to one point, or perhaps you can "see" the veins crossing. Then you might find that when you're talking with a friend about their house, you can go there in your mind's eye and "see" the veins. Then on to houses where you've never even been to physically....

In healing, this level of dowsing is also an asset. Your hands just know where to go. You can "see" where the problem is, just as you can feel and see the Light as it does Her/His work. It's just knowing.

It is in Ceremony at a sacred space where I have found my best connections with the spiritual realms. I may use dowsing tools to find the power center in the first place, as a way of tuning in, but once the ceremony starts, I put away my tools. Dowsing is a bridge to the other side, but you have to leave your tools if you want to see more than the spiritual shore-line. So go for deviceless!

so
go
slowly
and softly
into these things.
Dowsing is a tool that can
open us up to realms that we've
only dreamed of where we
are indeed
strangers
in a
strange
land.

But what a land!

Somehow each of us

must find ways to bring ourselves, our countries, this
Earth of ours back into balance. We must find
new/old ways of relating to each other.
New/old doors must be (re)opened,
and a synthesis of
Western Man
and
The Goddess
will be found
by each one of us

Glossary

ARCHEOASTRONOMY/ASTROARCHAEOLOGY
American/British terms for the study of alignments from sacred sites to significant horizonal astronomical events like the Summer Solstice Sunrise alignment at Stonehenge.

DOME – (Known in Britain as a *blind spring*). Primary water forced up under pressure towards the surface of the Earth. At some point, it hits an impermeable layer of rock or clay, and then moves laterally into veins.

EARTH ENERGIES – The life force system of our Earth. The equivalent to the human body's acupuncture meridians.

EARTH MOTHER – While the Mother and Father are everywhere, this term is used to identify those yin energies that are allowed to reach the surface of the Earth because of veins of water, fault lines and certain mineral deposits. Also refers to Gaia, the Greek deity, who was the Mother of us all.

ENERGY LEY – A six to eight-foot wide beam of yang energy with a direction of flow. Energy leys (E Leys) expand and contract according to the time of day, time of year, phase of Moon and other factors. They always runs in straight lines, and often, but not always, run concurrently with ley lines.

EQUINOX – The time when the Sun crosses the Equator making the night equal in length to the day.

GEOMANCY – The art of designing and placing structures in the landscape so that the Earth Energies enhance their intended use, and so that structure itself is in harmony with its environment.

LEY LINE – An alignment of sacred sites, each of which has primary water under it.

MAJOR AXIS – The most significant alignment of a sacred site. Usually the longest axis. At Stonehenge, it is the alignment to the Summer Solstice Sunrise.

MINOR AXIS – Any significant line drawn perpendicular to the major axis of a sacred site.

NEO-GEOMANCY – A partial and warped attempt to use the Earth Energies to gain political power over others. A misuse of these Energies.

POWER CENTER – At a minimum, the crossing of one energy ley and one vein of primary water.

PRIMARY WATER – (Also called *juvenile water*). Created in the bowels of the Earth as a biproduct of various chemical reactions. Does not come from rain water that has soaked into the Earth.

PSEUDO-GEOMANCY – False geomancy. Not in harmony with/ aware of the Earth Energies.

RANGE LINES – Synonymous with *ley line*. First used by William Pidgeon in 1853 in his book, *De-Coo-Dah*.

SARSEN – A kind of stone found on the Wiltshire downs. Used both at Stonehenge and at Avebury.

SOLAR FATHER – While the Father and the Mother are everywhere, this term is used to identify the yang energies, like energy leys, that seem to come from the Sun.

SOLSTICE – The times when the Sun reaches its maximum distance from the Equator. Summer Solstice occurs when it reaches the Tropic of Cancer; Winter Solstice, when it reaches the Tropic of Capricorn.

VEIN (of water) – cracks or fissure in the Earth's mantle that allow primary water to flow through them.

YANG – Active. Positive (+) polarity.

YIN – Receptive. Negative (–) polarity.

Selected Bibliography

Ashe, Geoffrey. 1977. *The Ancient Wisdom*. London: Macmillan.

Brennan, Martin. 1980. *The Boyne Valley Vision*. Portolaoise, Ireland: The Dolmen Press.

_____. 1983. *The Stars and the Stones*. London: Thames & Hudson.

Bird, Christopher. Aug 1973. "Dowsing in the U.S.A.: History, Past Achievements & Current Research". Danville, Vermont: *Digest of the American Society of Dowsers*. Vol 13, No 3, pp 105 to 120.

Bloom, William & Marko Pogacnik. 1985. *Ley Lines and Ecology*. Glastonbury: Gothic Image Publications.

Devereux, Paul and Ian Thompson. 1979. *The Ley Hunter's Companion*. London: Thames & Hudson.

_____. 1982. *Earthlights*. Wellingborough, Northamptonshire: Turnstone Press.

Graves, Tom. 1976. *Dowsing: Techniques and Applications*. London: Turnstone. (published in the U.S. and reprinted in the U.K. in 1986 as *The Diviner's Handbook*.)

_____. (Editor). 1980. *Dowsing and Archaeology*. Wellingborough, Northamptonshire: Turnstone Books.

_____. 1986. *Needles Of Stone Revisited*. Glastonbury: Gothic Image. © 1978.

Harvalik, Zaboj. Aug 1983. "High Frequency Beams Aid Locating the Dowsing Sensors". Danville, Vermont: *Digest of the American Society of Dowsers*. Vol 23, No 3.

Hester, Ben G. 1982. *Dowsing – An Exposé of Hidden Occult Forces*. Payson, Arizona, U.S.A.: Leaves of Autumn Books. (Copies may be obtained from the author at 4883 Hedrick Avenue, Arlington, California 92505, for $6.95 plus $1.00 postage.)

Howard-Gordon, Frances. 1982. *Glastonbury – Maker of Myths*. Glastonbury: Gothic Image Publications.

Hüser, Karl. 1982. *Wewelsburg 1933 bis 1945 – Kult und Terrorstätte Der SS (Eine Dokumentation)*. Verlag Bonifatius, Druckerei Paderborn.

Jaynes, Julian. 1976. *The Origin of Consciousness in the Breakdown of the Bicameral Mind*. Boston: Houghton Mifflin Company.

Larkman, Brian & Philip Heselton. 1985. *Earth Mysteries: An Exploratory*

Introduction. 170 Victoria Avenue, Hull, HU5 3DY, U.K.: The Northern Earth Mysteries Group.

Lonegren, Sig. 1985. *Earth Mysteries Handbook: Wholistic Non-intrusive Data Gathering Techniques.* Danville, Vermont: American Society of Dowsers.

Mavor, James W. Jr. & Byron Dix. Dec 1983. "New England Stone Mounds As Ritual Architecture." Rowley, Massachusetts: *Bulletin of the Early Sites Research Society Society.* Vol 10, No2.

Michell, John. 1974. *Flying Saucer Vision.* London: Sphere Books Ltd. © 1969

_____. 1975. *Earth Spirit.* London: Thames & Hudson.

_____. 1975. *View Over Atlantis.* London: Garnstone Press Ltd. © 1969.

_____.1979. *The Old Stones of Land's End.* Bristol, England: Pentacle Books. © 1974.

_____. 1983. *The New View Over Atlantis.* London: Thames & Hudson. © 1969.

Pagels, Elaine. 1981. *The Gnostic Gospels.* New York: Vantage Books. © 1979.

Pennick, Nigel. 1981. *Hitler's Secret Sciences.* Suffolk, England: Neville Spearman.

Pidgeon, William. 1853. *Traditions of De-Coo-Dah.* New York: Bridgman and Fanning.

Robbins, Don. 1985. *Circles of Silence.* London: Souvenir Press.

Ross, Terry. May 1983. "A Dowser's Model." Danville, Vermont: *The Digest of the American Society of Dowsers.* Vol 23 No.2, pp 11-14.

Starhawk. 1982. *Dreaming the Dark: Magic, Sex and Politics.* Boston, U.S.: Beacon Press.

Teudt, Wilhelm. 1917. *Deutsche Sachlichkeit.* Berlin.

_____. 1929. *Germanische Heiligtümer.* Jena.

Underwood, Guy. 1973. *The Pattern of the Past.* New York: Abelard-Shuman, Ltd. © 1969.

Watkins, Alfred. 1977. *The Old Straight Track.* London: Abacus. © 1925.

Williamson, Tom & Liz Bellamy. 1983. *Ley Lines In Question.* Kingswood, Tadworth, Surrey: World's Work.

Yogananda, Paramahansa. *Autobiography of a Yogi.* London: Century Publishing Co.

Publications

The American Dowser, American Society of Dowsers, Danville, Vermont 05828, U.S.A. Dowsing, some on Earth Mysteries.

The Journal of the British Society of Dowsers, Sycamore Cottage, Tamley Lane, Hastingleigh, Ashford, Kent, U.K. Dowsing, some on Earth Mysteries.

Caerdroia, 52 Thundersley Grove, Thundersley, Benfleet, Essex, U.K. Labyrinths and mazes.

Bulletin of the Early Sites Research Society, Long Hill, Rowley, Massachusetts 01969, U.S.A. $20.00 a year. Unexplained New England archaeology.

Glastonbury Communicator, The Assembly Rooms, High Street, Glastonbury, Somerset BA6 9DU, U.K. Some Earth Mysteries. Information on EM Gatherings.

New England Antiquities Research Association Journal, NEARA Membership, Betty Lewis, 172 Robin Hill Road, Chelmsford, Mass. 01824, U.S.A. $20.00 a year. The New England stone chamber controversy. Some Native American material.

Stonehenge Viewpoint, 2821 De La Vina Street, Santa Barbara, California 93105 U.S.A. $10.00 for 10 issues. The EM book catalog is worth the price of the subscription alone.

The Ley Hunter, PO Box 5, Brecon, Powys, Wales. £4.00 U.K.; Overseas $20.00 (air); $15.00 (surface); £6.00 (Europe). Magazine of the Earth Mysteries.

The Pipes of P.A.N., Pagans Against Nukes, 'Blaenberem', Mynyddcerrig, Llanelli, Dyfed, Cymru (Wales) SA15 5BL. U.K. £2.50 + 50p per person P.A.N. membership fee; Overseas £7.00 (air); £4.00 (surface). Overseas payments should be made in Sterling Drafts drawn in London.

Tapes

Custer Died For Your Sins. Floyd Westerman. From Red Crow Productions, P.O. Box 49, Innchelium, Washington 99138, U.S.A.

Dancing Circles — Tape 1. Colin Harrison, 51 Hill Head, Glastonbury, Somerset, U.K.. Music by the Dove Workshop. Comes with instruction manual for beginner circle dancers.

The Glass Isle. Michael Law. Synfinity, The Chapel House, Perch Hill, Westbury-Sub-Mendip, Nr. Wells, Somerset BA5 1JA, U.K. Avalonian music of the spheres.

Magical Ring. Clannad. Tara Records, 5 Tara Street, Dublin 2, Ireland. Music for sacred spaces.

Second Chants. Prana. Tangelynen, CwmCou, Newcastle Emlyn, Dyfed, Wales, U.K. Good Earth Mother chants for ceremonies.

Many of these books and tapes mentioned above are available from: Gothic Image Ltd., 7 High Street, Glastonbury, Somerset BA6 9DP, U.K. Write for their catalog.

Dowsing Supplies

The American Society of Dowsers, Danville, Vermont 05828, U.S.A.
The British Society of Dowsers, Sycamore Cottage, Tamley
    Lane, Hastingleigh, Ashford, Kent, U.K.
The Gothic Image Ltd., 7 High Street, Glastonbury, Somerset BA6 9DP, U.K.

The Bach Flower Remedies

In Britain: Bach Flower Remedies Ltd., Dr. E. Bach Centre, Mount Vernon, Sotwell, Wallingford, Oxon., OX10 0PZ, U.K.
In USA/Canada: Ellon (Bach USA) Inc., P.O. Box 320, Woodmere, N.Y., 11598, U.S.A.

Gothic Image Tours

If you are feeling ready to visit some truly ancient sacred sites, Sig Lonegren leads tours/pilgrimages with Jamie George and Frances Howard-Gordon of Gothic Image to megalithic Britain and Ireland. Similar trips in the future are planned for France and Russia. For further information contact Gothic Image Tours, 7 High Street, Glastonbury, Somerset BA6 9DP, U.K.

If you wish to contact the author, his address is:
Sig Lonegren, Box 218, Greensboro, Vermont 05841, U.S.A.

Gothic Image Publications

We are a Glastonbury based Imprint dedicated to publishing books and pamphlets which offer a new and radical approach to our perception of the world in which we live.

As ideas about the nature of life change, we aim to make available those new perspectives which clarify our understanding of ourselves and the Earth we share.

The Glastonbury Tor Maze	Geoffrey Ashe	£1.25
Ley Lines and Ecology An Introduction	William Bloom and Marko Pogacnik	£1.50
Devas, Fairies and Angels A Modern Approach	William Bloom	£2.50
Glastonbury – Maker of Myths	Frances Howard-Gordon	£3.95
Needles of Stone Revisited	Tom Graves	£5.95

These titles are available by Mail Order. Add 20% for postage and packing – 40% for air mail to USA and Canada.

Write for our Mail Order Catalogue enclosing an A5 sized stamped addressed envelope.

Gothic Image Publications
7 High Street,
Glastonbury,
Somerset BA6 9DP
ENGLAND
Telephone 0458 31453